Dinah Zike's

Big Book of
Science

Middle School & High School

Dinah Zike, M.Ed.

This book is dedicated to my parents,
Coney Harwood Dorough
and
Etta Catherine Bearden Dorough,
who encouraged my interest in science
by allowing me the freedom to
experiment, experience, and collect.
Thank you for filling my childhood years with
animals, plants, land, family and love.

Happy 50th Anniversary
August 4, 2001

Copyright ©2001, Dinah-Might Adventures, LP
Dinah-Might Adventures, LP
P.O. Box 690328
San Antonio, Texas 78269-0328

Office (210) 698-0123
Fax (210) 698-0095
Orders only: 1-800-99DINAH (993-4624)
Orders or catalog requests: orders@dinah.com
E-mail: dma@dinah.com
Website: www.dinah.com
ISBN Number: 1-882796-18-7

Dear Teacher,

Who, What, When, Why

In this book you will find instructions for making Foldables, as well as ideas on how to use them. You probably have seen at least one of the Foldables featured in this book used in supplemental programs or staff-deveopment workshops. Today, my Foldables are used internationally. I present workshops and keynotes to over fifty thousand teachers and parents a year, sharing the Foldables that I began inventing, designing, and adapting over thirty years ago. Around the world, students of all ages are using them for daily work, note-taking activities, student-directed projects, forms of alternative assessment, science-lab journals, quantitative and qualitative observation books, graphs, tables, and more.

Add and Amend

After workshop presentations, participants would ask me for lists of activities to be used with the Foldables they had just learned to make. They needed help visualizing how to convert science data into Foldables. So, over fifteen years ago, I began collecting and sharing the ideas listed in this book.

   Needless to say, there have been many advances in science since I first started these lists. Just recently, for example, students were studying the five kingdoms of living organisms, but today they learn there are six. I've tried to keep the lists updated, but I'm sure some of the thousands of things I've listed are already out of date. I've left spaces throughout the book for you to add your own ideas and activities, record new science information, and make amendments to my lists. It is good for students to experience the cause and effect of changing science data.

   I now hand these lists of ideas and information over to you and your students. Have fun adding and amending.

Workshops

For more information on Dinah Zike's workshops and keynote presentations, contact Cecil Stepman at **1-210-698-0123** or **cecil@ dinah.com.**

Orders

To receive a free catalog or to order other books by Dinah Zike, call **1-800-99DINAH** or e-mail at **orders@Dinah.com.**

E-Group

To join Dinah Zike's e-group and receive a new activity every month, send an e-mail to **mindy@dinah.com.**

Table of Contents

Why use Foldables in science?

When teachers ask me why they should take time to use the Foldables featured in this book, I explain that they

. . . quickly organize, display, and arrange data, making it easier for students to grasp science concepts, theories, processes, facts, and ideas. They also help sequence events as outlined in the content standards.

. . . result in student-made study guides that are compiled as students listen for main ideas, read for main ideas, or conduct research.

. . . provide a multitude of creative formats in which students can present projects, research, experiment results, and inquiry-based reports instead of typical poster board or science fair formats.

. . . replace teacher-generated writing or photocopied sheets with student-generated print.

. . . incorporate the use of such skills as comparing and contrasting, recognizing cause and effect, and finding similarities and differences into daily work and long-term projects. For example, these Foldables can be used to compare and contrast student explanations of inquiry-based questions to explanations currently accepted by scientists.

. . . continue to "immerse" students in previously learned vocabulary, concepts, generalizations, ideas, and theories, providing them with a strong foundation that they can build upon with new observations, concepts, and knowledge.

. . . can be used by students or teachers to easily communicate data through graphs, tables, charts, diagrams, models, and Venn diagrams.

. . . allow students to make their own journals for recording qualitative and quantitative observations.

. . . can be used as alternative assessment tools by teachers to evaluate student progress or by students to evaluate their own progress.

. . . integrate language arts, social sciences, and mathematics into the study of science.

. . . provide a sense of student ownership or investiture in the science curriculum.

Foldable Basics

What to Write and Where

Teach students to write general information—titles, vocabulary words, concepts, questions, main ideas, and laws or principles—on the front tabs of their Foldables. General information is viewed every time a student looks at a Foldable. Foldables help students focus on and remember key points without being distracted by other print.

Ask students to write specific information—supporting ideas, student thoughts, answers to questions, research information, empirical data, class notes, observations, and definitions—under the tabs.

As you teach, demonstrate different ways in which Foldables can be used. Soon you will find that students make their own Foldables and use them independently for study guides and projects.

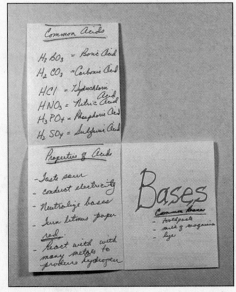

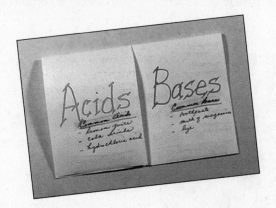

With or Without Tabs

Foldables with flaps or tabs create study guides that students can use to self check what they know about the general information on the front of tabs. Use Foldables without tabs for assessment purposes (where it's too late to self check) or projects where information is presented for others to view quickly.

Venn Diagram used as a study guide

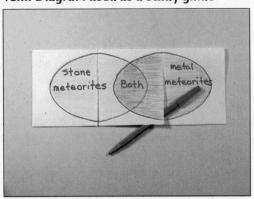

Venn Diagram used for assessment

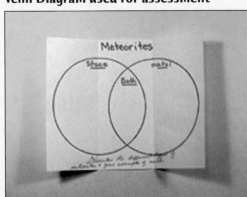

What to Do with Scissors and Glue

I do not ask middle school and high school students to carry glue and scissors from class to class. Instead, I set up a small table or rolling cart in the back of the classroom and provide a few containers of glue, several pairs of scissors (sometimes tied to the cart), containers of colored pencils, a stapler, and anything else I think students might need. Don't be surprised if students donate colored markers, decorative-edged scissors, gel pens, stencils, and other art items to your cart.

The more they make and use graphic organizers, the faster students become at producing them.

Storing Graphic Organizers in Student Portfolios

Turn one-gallon freezer bags into student portfolios. Students can carry their portfolios in their notebooks if they place strips of two-inch clear tape along one side and punch three holes through the taped edge.

Have each student write his or her name, period, and class along the top of the plastic portfolio with a permanent marker and cover the writing with two-inch clear tape to keep it from wearing off.

Cut the bottom corners off the bag so it won't hold air and will stack and store easily.

> **HINT**: *I found it more convenient to keep student portfolios in my classroom so student work was always available when needed and not "left in a locker" or "at home." Giant laundry-soap boxes make good storage containers for portfolios, and it isn't difficult to get one for each period.*

Let Students Use This Book As an Idea Reference

Make this book of lists available to students to use as an idea reference for projects, discussions, science debates, extra credit work, cooperative learning group presentations, and more.

Selecting the Appropriate Foldable

Dividing Science Concepts into Parts

Foldables divide information and make it visual. In order to select the appropriate Foldable, decide how many parts you want to divide the information into and then determine which Foldable best illustrates or fits those parts. Foldables that are three-dimensional also make the student interact with the data kinesthetically.

For example, if you are studying the three kinds of rocks, you could choose a foldable that has three tabs (or sections), write *igneous, metamorphic,* and *sedimentary* on the front tabs, and place information and examples of each type of rock under the tabs.

Science Concepts Already Divided into Parts								
Earth			**Life**			**Physical**		
Parts	**Science Concept**		**Parts**	**Science Concept**		**Parts**	**Science Concept**	
10	Mohs Scale		13	Vitamins		4	States of Matter	
4	Layers of Earth		2	Sexual and Asexual		3	Classes of Levers	
3	Eras of Geologic Time		2	Monocots and Dicots		2	Kinetic and Potential Energy	
9	Solar System Planets		2	Endotherms and Ectotherms		2	Direct and Alternating Current	
5	Layers of the Atmosphere		6	Kingdoms of Living Organisms		3	Newton's Three Laws of Motion	
4	Reduce, Reuse, Recycle, Refuse		2	Angiosperms and Gymnosperms		2	Static Fluids and Fluids in Motion	
3	Igneous, Metamorphic, Sedimentary Rock		2	Vascular and Nonvascular Plants		3	Conduction, Convection, Radiation	
			3	Skeletal, Smooth, and Cardiac Muscles		2	Balanced and Unbalanced Forces	
			3	Producer, Consumer, Decomposer				

Science Concepts That Can Be Divided into Parts		
Earth	*Life*	*Physical*
Air Pressure	A Life Cycle	Forces
Earth's Plates	Examples of Fungi	Radiant Energy
Causes of Erosion	Parts of a Plant Cell	Types of Friction
Formation of a Fossil	Arachnid Identification	Kinds of Batteries
Effects of Ocean Movement	Human Digestive System	Examples of Inertia
Weather Patterns over Time	Levels of Life in the Ocean	The Movement of Light
The Sun as an Energy Source	Characteristics of Invertebrates	Properties of Magnetism
Convection Current Within Earth	Ways in Which Animals Reproduce	Physical Properties of Matter
		Law of Conservation of Mass and Energy

Dividing Skills and Foldables into Parts

Reading, writing, and thinking skills can easily be used with Foldables. The following lists show examples of skills and activities and a selection of Foldables divided into parts. You may want to refer to this page as you select activities from the lists of science topics in the third section of this book (see pages 46–159).

Skills and Activities Divided into Parts	
1 Part	**2 Parts**
Find the Main Idea	Compare and Contrast
Predict an Outcome	Cause and Effect
Narrative Science Writing	Similarities and Differences
Descriptive Science Writing	Pros and Cons
Expository Science Writing	Facts and Opinions
Persuasive Science Writing	Form and Function
3 Parts	**4 Parts**
Venn Diagrams	Who, What, When, Where
Know?-Like to Know?-Learned?	What, Where, When, Why/How
Past, Present, Future	
Beginning, Middle, End	
Any Number of Parts	
Questioning	Making and Using Tables
Flow Charts	Making and Using Graphs
Vocabulary Words	Sequencing Data or Events
Concept Webs or Maps	

Foldables Divided into Parts	
1 Part	**2 Parts**
Half Book	Two-Tab Book
Folded Book	Pocket Book
Three-Quarter Book	Shutterfold
Large Matchbook	Matchbook Cut in Half
Bound Book	Concept Map with Two Tabs
3 Parts	**4 Parts**
Trifold Book	Four-Tab Book
Three-Tab Book	Standing Cube
Pyramid Book	Top-Tab Book
Layered-Look Book	Four-Door Book
Any Number of Parts	
Accordion Book	Circle Graph
Pop-Up Book	Concept-Map Book
Sentence-Strip Holder	Vocabulary Book
Folded Table, Chart, or Graph	Time-Line Book
Pyramid Mobile	Bound Book
Multiple-Pocket Books	Layered-Look Book (three or more sheets of paper)

Using Visuals and Graphics with Foldables

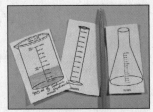

I designed the graphics on pages 8–11 to be used as visual aids for student production, while immersing students in measurement, geography, and history. At times, I require these graphics to be used in student presentations. I photocopy them or print them from my computer and pass them out. At other times, students incorporate them into their journals, notes, projects, and study guides independently. I found that students were more likely to use graphics if they were available on a classroom computer where they could be selected and printed out as needed.

1. Give students small pictures of beakers, cylinders, and flasks and ask them to color in the volume of liquid used in an experiment. This forces every student in a group to be involved in measurement, not just the student who is doing the actual measuring. Include these measurement aids in projects and journals.

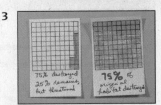

2. Mark and label maps to show where specific science events occurred, where a famous scientist worked, where a plant or animal's habitat is located, where fossils have been found, where volcanoes are active, etc.

3. Hundreds grids can be used to illustrate percentages, decimals, and bar graphs.

4. Use time lines to record when someone lived or when an event or sequence of events occurred. Use two timelines to compare what was happening in two different areas at the same time.

5. Use small picture frames to sketch or name a person, place, or thing. Great to use the four-door book as a "who, what, when, where" activity.

6. Make clocks available for students to record when something starts and stops. The clocks can be glued onto graphic organizers or observation journals. Many of the middle school students I see can't tell time unless it is digital. These graphics provide much needed practice.

7. Use rain gauges and thermometers in projects to record average precipitation amounts or average seasonal temperatures of a given habitat or biome.

8. Use thermometers to record qualitative data such as melting points and temperatures.

> **NOTE:** *I grant you permission to photocopy these pages and place copies of them in the production center or publishing center of your classroom. I also grant you permission to scan these pages and use them electronically.*

Reproducible Science Graphics

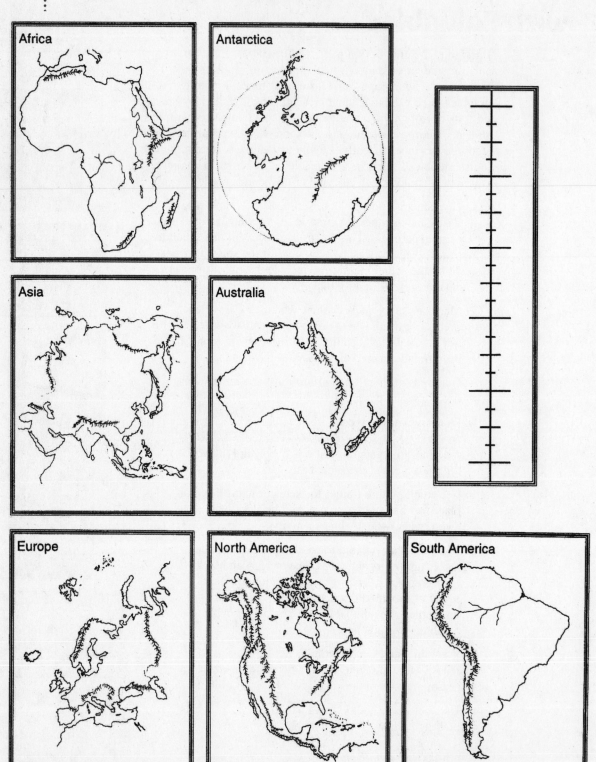

Reproducible Science Graphics

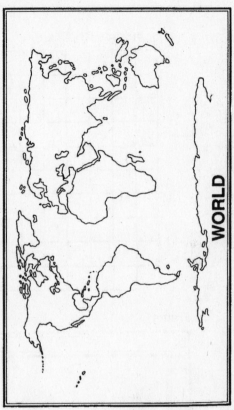

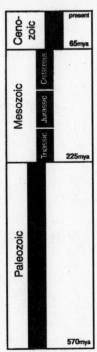

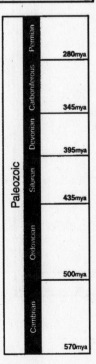

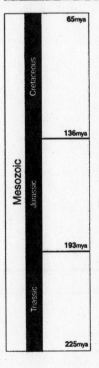

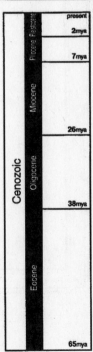

Reproducible Science Graphics

Hundreds Grid

Frame

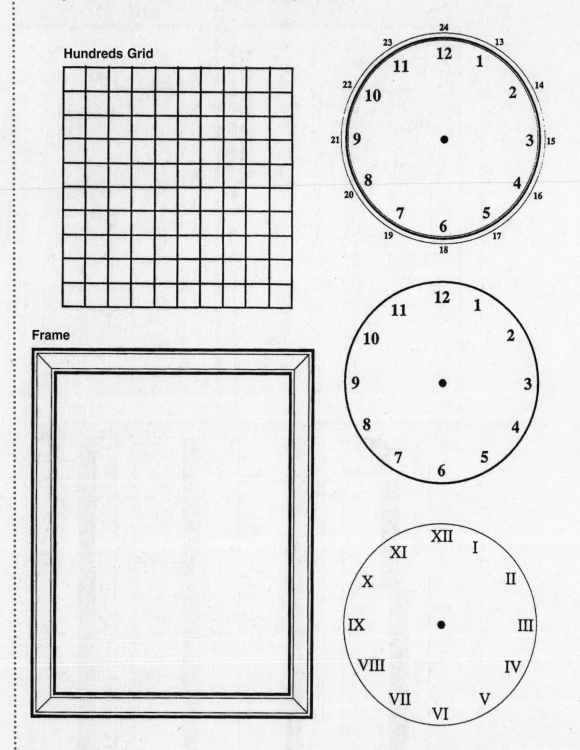

Reproducible Science Graphics

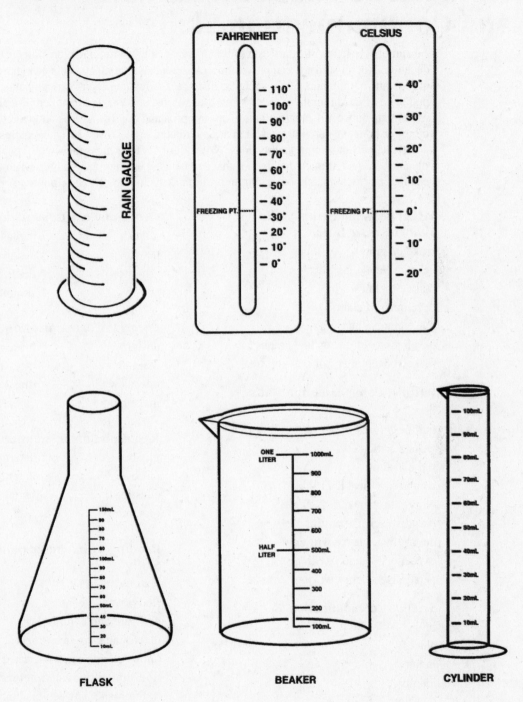

FLASK

BEAKER

CYLINDER

National Science Standards and Communication Skills

The National Science Standards stress the importance of communication skills in science education. Not all students can or will become scientists, but all students can learn to think, analyze, and communicate in a scientific manner. Throughout their lives, students will be called upon to be science literate as they make observations, analyze and recall empirical data, read and differentiate between fact and opinion, discuss pros and cons of actions and reactions, justify voting for or against an issue, research a topic related to their well being or interests, make cause-and-effect decisions about their actions, write editorials to express their views publicly, and more. Foldables are one of many techniques that can be used to integrate reading, writing, thinking, debating, researching, and other communication skills into an interdisciplinary science curriculum.

Visual Communication Skills That Organize Data

make diagrams
develop Venn diagrams
make timelines
develop flow charts
make charts and/or tables
develop bar, circle, or line graphs
make concept maps or network trees

Writing/Communication Skills

list
outline
write a critique
write a summary
record empirical data
write interview questions
narrative science writing
descriptive science writing
expository science writing
persuasive science writing

Science Communication Skills

infer
classify
inquire
identify
question
measure
investigate
hypothesize
interpret data
design experiments
determine form and function
make qualitative/quantitative observations

Oral Language Communication Skills

relate   explain
debate   discuss
critique   describe
review   summarize

Creative Communication Skills

design   make a mobile
diagram   make a diorama
interview   illustrate and label
make models   complete a project

Research Communication Skills

inquire   determine
discover   investigate
question   search the Internet
research

Reading/Thinking Communication Skills

read for main idea
find pros and cons
compare and contrast
determine cause and effect
know?-like to know?-learned?
find similarities and differences
differentiate between fact and opinion

Basic Foldable Shapes

The following figures illustrate the basic folds that are referred to throughout the following section of this book (pgs. 14–44).

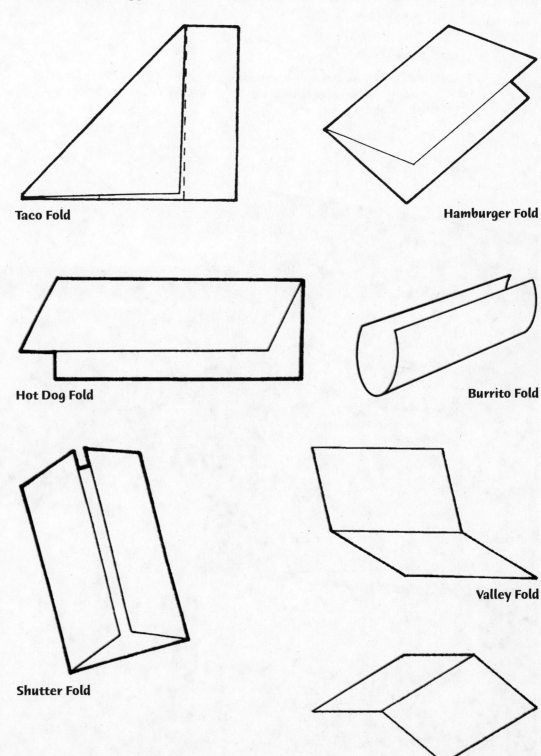

Taco Fold

Hamburger Fold

Hot Dog Fold

Burrito Fold

Shutter Fold

Valley Fold

Mountain Fold

Half-Book

Fold a sheet of paper (8 1/2" x 11") in half.

1. This book can be folded vertically like a *hot dog* or . . .

2. . . . it can be folded horizontally like a *hamburger.*

Use this book for descriptive, expository, persuasive, or narrative science writing, as well as graphs, diagrams, or charts.

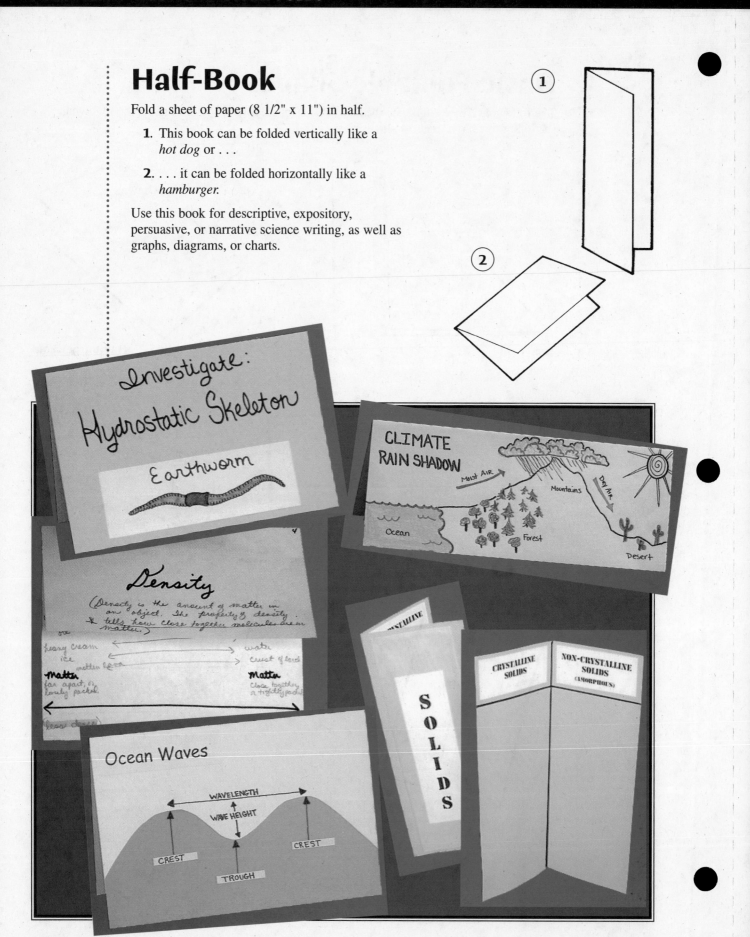

Folded Book

1. Make a *half-book.* (see pg. 14)

2. Fold it in half again like a *hamburger.* This makes a ready-made cover, and two small pages for information on the inside.

Use photocopied work sheets, Internet print outs, and student-drawn diagrams or maps to make this book. One sheet of paper becomes two activities and two grades.

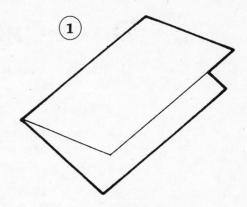

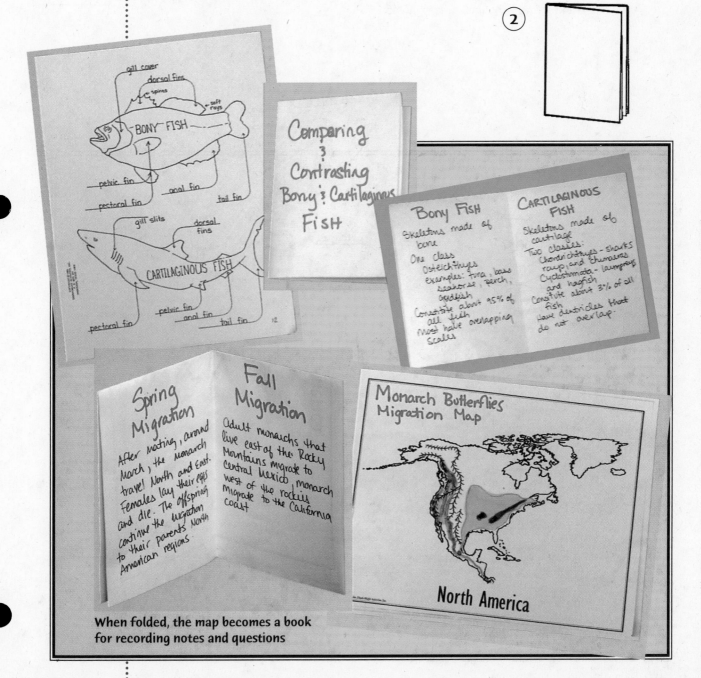

When folded, the map becomes a book for recording notes and questions

Three-Quarter Book

1. Take a *two-tab* book (see pg. 18) and raise the left-hand tab.

2. Cut the tab off at the top fold line.

3. A larger book of information can be made by gluing several *three-quarter books* side-by-side.

Sketch or glue a graphic to the left, write one or more questions on the right, and record answers and information under the right tab.

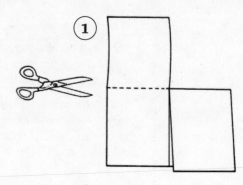

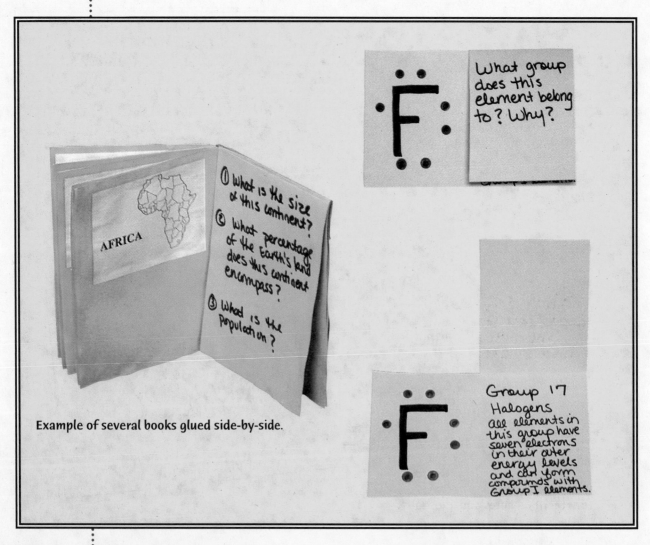

Example of several books glued side-by-side.

Bound Book

1. Take two sheets of paper (8 1/2" × 11") and separately fold them like a *hamburger*. Place the papers on top of each other, leaving one sixteenth of an inch between the *mountain tops*.

2. Mark both folds one inch from the outer edges.

3. On one of the folded sheets, cut from the top and bottom edge to the marked spot on both sides.

4. On the second folded sheet, start at one of the marked spots and cut the fold between the two marks.

5. Take the cut sheet from step 3 and fold it like a *burrito*. Place the *burrito* through the other sheet and then open the *burrito*. Fold the bound pages in half to form an eight-page book.

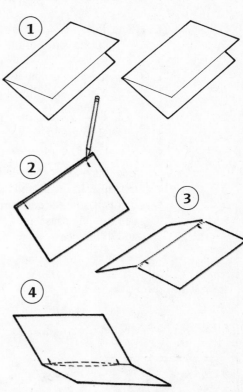

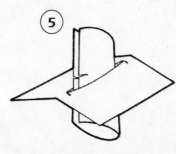

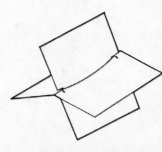

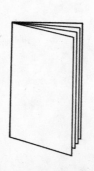

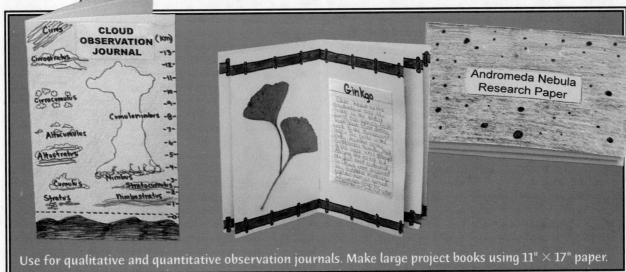

Use for qualitative and quantitative observation journals. Make large project books using 11" × 17" paper.

Two-Tab Book

1. Take a *folded book* (see pg. 15) and cut up the *valley* of the inside fold toward the *mountain top*. This cut forms two large tabs that can be used front and back for writing and illustrations.

2. The book can be expanded by making several of these folds and gluing them side-by-side.

Use this book with data occurring in twos. For example, list acids and bases or monocots and dicots. Use it for comparing and contrasting, determining cause and effect, finding similarities and differences, and more.

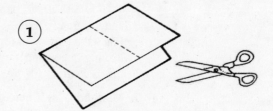

①

②

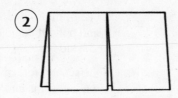

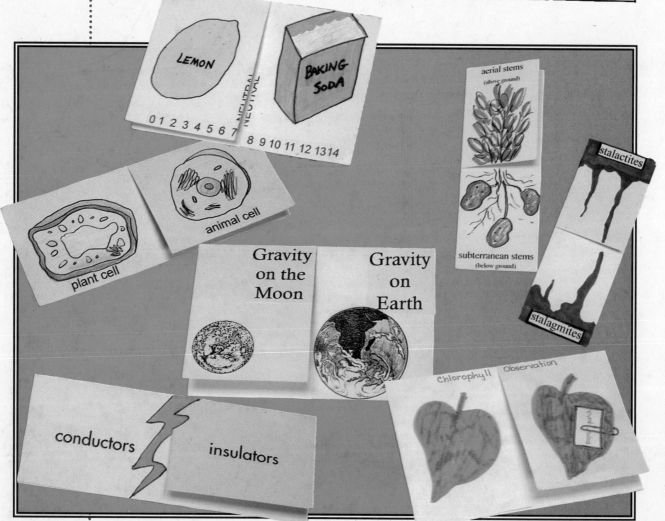

Pocket Book

1. Fold a sheet of paper (8 1/2" × 11") in half like a *hamburger*.

2. Open the folded paper and fold one of the long sides up two inches to form a pocket. Refold along the *hamburger* fold so that the newly formed pockets are on the inside.

3. Glue the outer edges of the two-inch fold with a small amount of glue.

4. **Optional:** Glue a cover around the *pocket book*.

   Variation: Make a multi-paged booklet by gluing several pockets side-by-side. Glue a cover around the multi-paged *pocket book*.

Use 3" × 5" index cards inside the pockets. Store student-made books, such as two-tab books and folded books in the pockets.

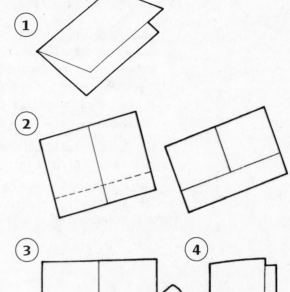

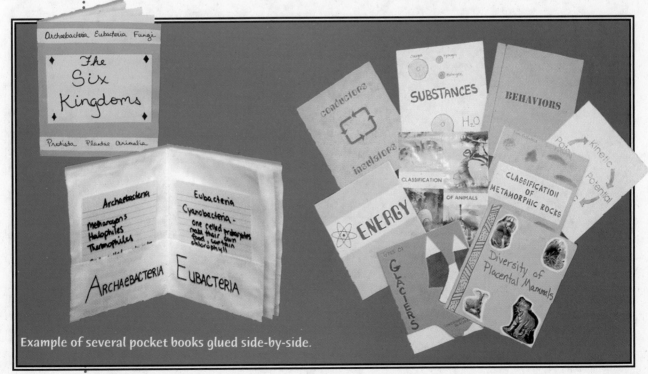

Example of several pocket books glued side-by-side.

Matchbook

1. Fold a sheet of paper (8 1/2" × 11") like a *hamburger,* but fold it so that one side is one inch longer than the other side.

2. Fold the one-inch tab over the short side forming an envelopelike fold.

3. Cut the front flap in half toward the *mountain top* to create two flaps.

Use this book to report on one thing, such as one element, or for reporting on two things, such as the cause and effect of soil erosion.

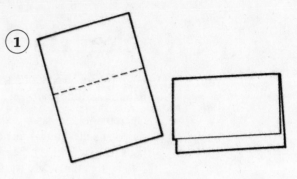

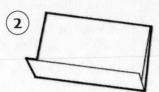

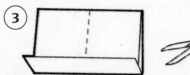

Actual size approximately 6 ft. × 4 ft.

Use large matchbooks to make a giant periodic table of elements for your classroom.

Shutter Fold

1. Begin as if you were going to make a *hamburger* but instead of creasing the paper, pinch it to show the midpoint.

2. Fold the outer edges of the paper to meet at the pinch, or mid-point, forming a *shutter fold.*

Use this book for data occurring in twos. Or, make this fold using 11" × 17" paper and smaller books—such as the half book, journal, and two-tab book—that can be glued inside to create a large project full of student work.

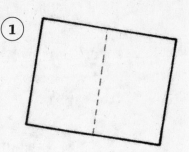

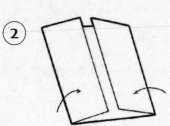

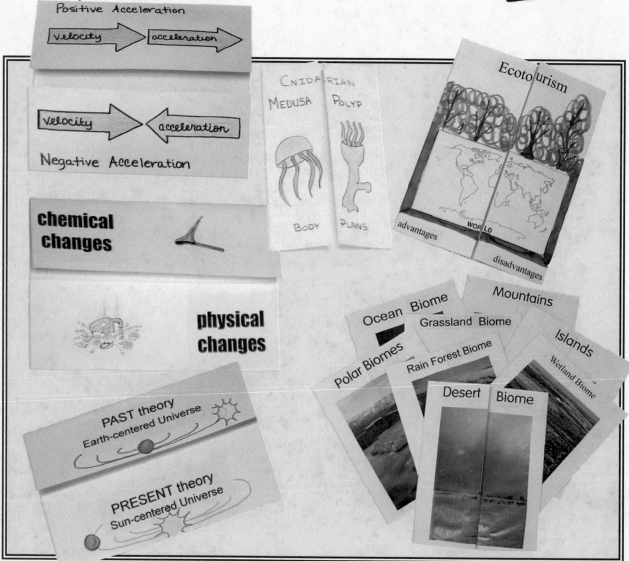

Trifold Book

1. Fold a sheet of paper (8 1/2" × 11") into thirds.

2. Use this book as is, or cut into shapes. If the trifold is cut, leave plenty of fold on both sides of the designed shape, so the book will open and close in three sections. (See Earth example below.)

Use this book to make charts with three columns or rows, large Venn diagrams, reports on data occurring in threes, or to show the outside and inside of something and to write about it.

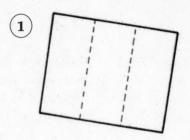

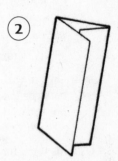

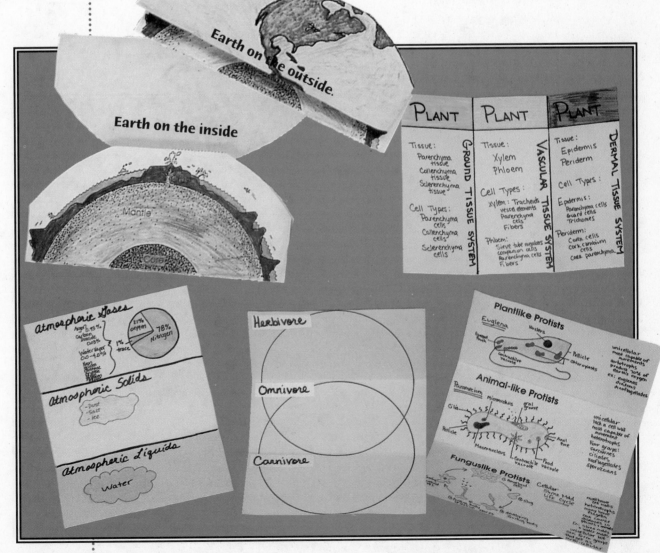

Earth on the outside.

Earth on the inside

Three-Tab Book

1. Fold a sheet of paper like a *hot dog*.

2. With the paper horizontal, and the fold of the *hot dog* up, fold the right side toward the center, trying to cover one half of the paper.

   NOTE: *If you fold the right edge over first, the final graphic organizer will open and close like a book.*

3. Fold the left side over the right side to make a book with three folds.

4. Open the folded book. Place your hands between the two thicknesses of paper and cut up the two *valleys* on one side only. This will form three tabs.

Use this book for data occurring in threes, and for two-part Venn diagrams.

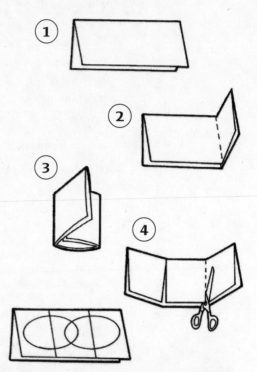

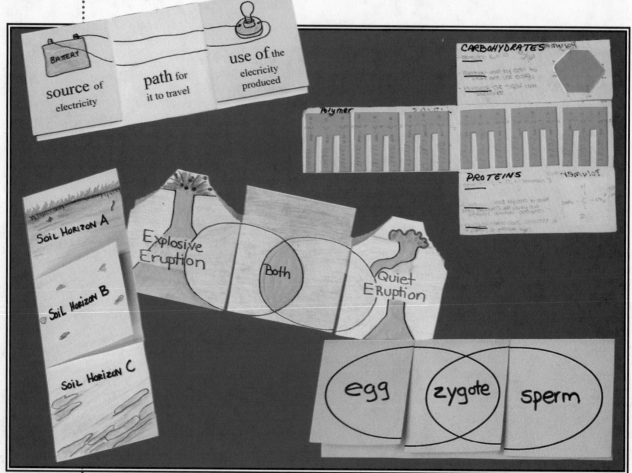

Pyramid Fold

1. Fold a sheet of paper (8 1/2" × 11") into a *taco,* forming a square. Cut off the excess rectangular tab formed by the fold.

2. Open the folded *taco* and refold it the opposite way forming another *taco* and an X-fold pattern.

3. Cut one of the folds to the center of the X, or the midpoint, and stop. This forms two triangular-shaped flaps.

4. Glue one of the flaps under the other, forming a *pyramid.*

5. Label front sections and write information, notes, thoughts, and questions inside the pyramid on the back of the appropriate tab.

Use to make mobiles and dioramas.
Use with data occurring in threes.

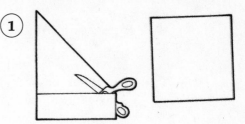

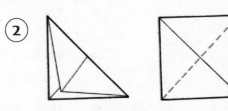

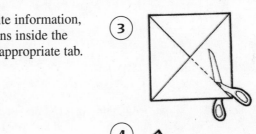

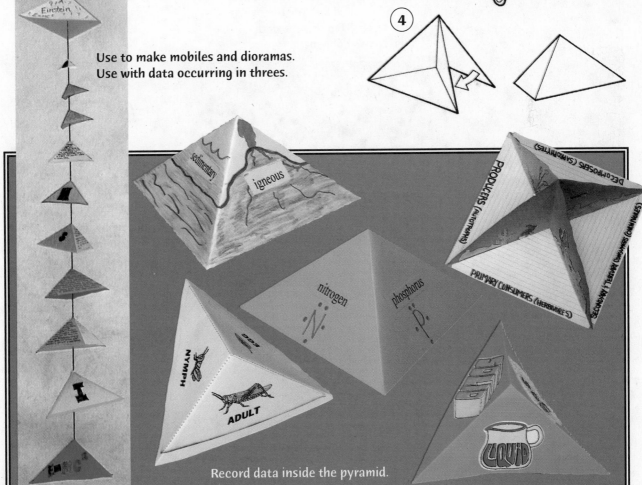

Record data inside the pyramid.

Layered-Look Book

1. Stack two sheets of paper (8 1/2" × 11") so that the back sheet is one inch higher than the front sheet.

2. Bring the bottom of both sheets upward and align the edges so that all of the layers or tabs are the same distance apart.

3. When all tabs are an equal distance apart, fold the papers and crease well.

4. Open the papers and glue them together along the *valley* or inner center fold or, staple them along the mountain.

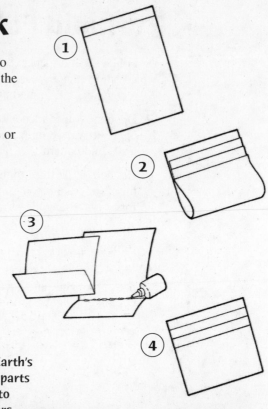

Make one layered book for Earth's atmosphere and one for the parts of Earth. Overlap the books to show Earth's concentric layers.

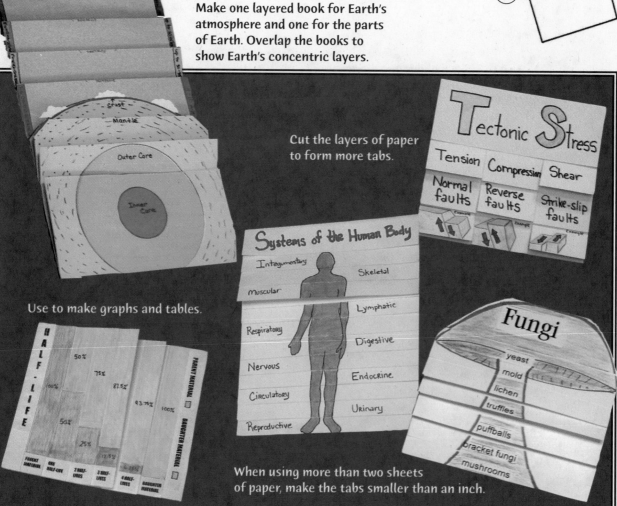

Cut the layers of paper to form more tabs.

Use to make graphs and tables.

When using more than two sheets of paper, make the tabs smaller than an inch.

Four-Tab Book

1. Fold a sheet of paper (8 1/2" × 11") in half like a *hot dog*.

2. Fold this long rectangle in half like a *hamburger*.

3. Fold both ends back to touch the *mountain top* or fold it like an *accordion*.

4. On the side with two *valleys* and one *mountain top*, make vertical cuts through one thickness of paper, forming four tabs.

Use this book for data occurring in fours. For example: continental land, ocean shelf, ocean slope, and ocean floor.

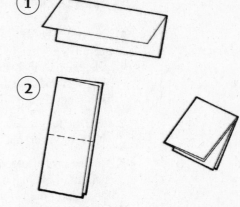

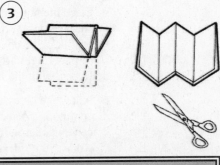

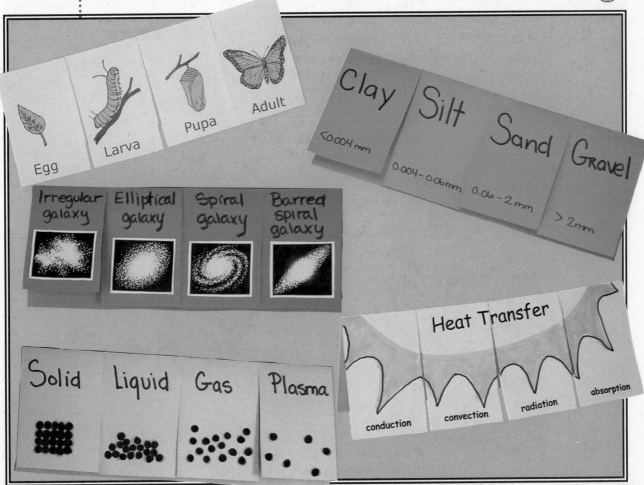

Standing Cube

1. Use two sheets of the same size paper. Fold each like a *hamburger*. However, fold one side one half inch shorter than the other side. This will make a tab that extends out one half inch on one side.

2. Fold the long side over the short side of both sheets of paper, making tabs.

3. On one of the folded papers, place a small amount of glue along the the small folded tab, next to the *valley* but not in it.

4. Place the non-folded edge of the second sheet of paper square into the *valley* and fold the glue-covered tab over this sheet of paper. Press flat until the glue holds. Repeat with the other side.

5. Allow the glue to dry completely before continuing. After the glue has dried, the cube can be collapsed flat to allow students to work at their desks. The cube can also be folded into fourths for easier storage, or for moving it to a display area.

Use with data occurring in fours or make it into a project. Make a small display cube using 8 1/2" × 11" paper. Use 11" × 17" paper to make large project cubes that you can glue other books onto for display. Notebook paper, photocopied sheets, magazine pictures, and current events also can be displayed on the large cube.

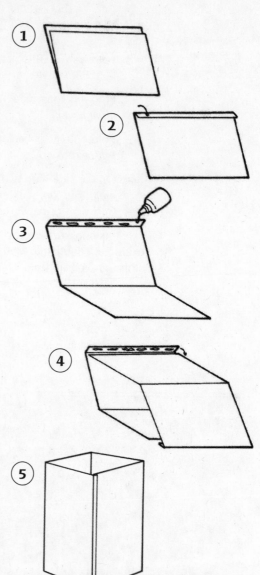

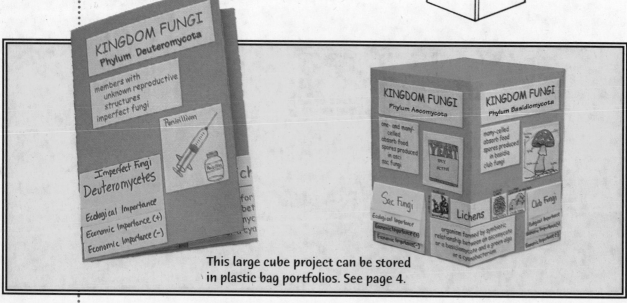

This large cube project can be stored in plastic bag portfolios. See page 4.

Four-Door Book

1. Make a *shutter fold* (see pg. 22) using 11" × 17" or 12" × 18" paper.

2. Fold the *shutter fold* in half like a *hamburger.* Crease well.

3. Open the project and cut along the two inside *valley* folds.

4. These cuts will form four doors on the inside of the project.

Use this fold for data occurring in fours. When folded in half like a *hamburger,* a finished *four-door book* can be glued inside a large (11" × 17") *shutter fold* as part of a larger project.

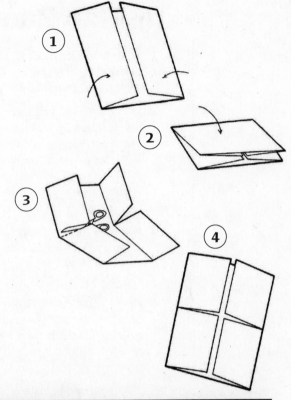

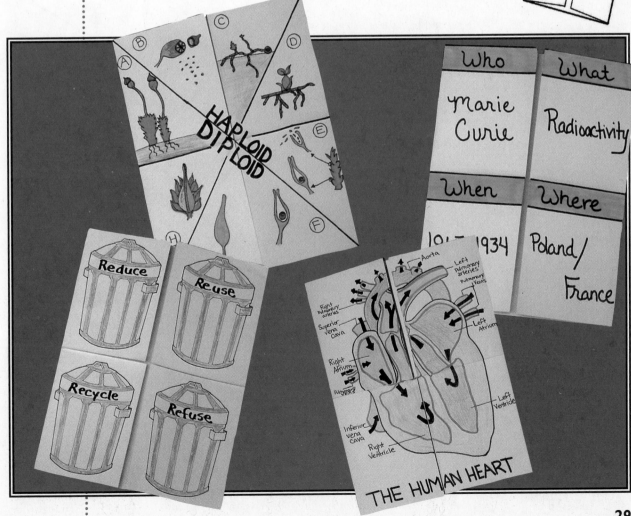

Top-Tab Book

1. Fold a sheet of paper (8 1/2" × 11") in half like a *hamburger.* Cut the center fold, forming two half sheets.

2. Fold one of the half sheets four times. Begin by folding in half like a *hamburger,* fold again like a *hamburger,* and finally again like a *hamburger.* This folding has formed your pattern of four rows and four columns, or 16 small squares.

3. Fold two sheets of paper (8 1/2" × 11") in half like a *hamburger.* Cut the center folds, forming four half sheets.

4. Hold the pattern vertically and place on a half sheet of paper under the pattern. Cut the bottom right hand square out of both sheets. Set this first page aside.

5. Take a second half sheet of paper and place it under the pattern. Cut the first and second right hand squares out of both sheets. Place the second page on top of the first page.

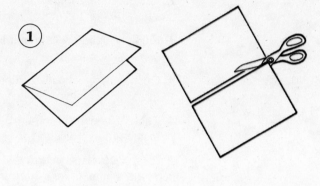

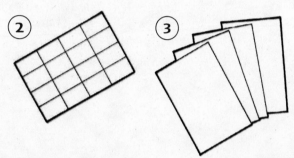

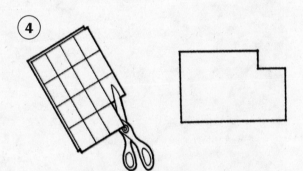

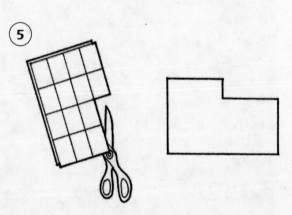

6. Take a third half sheet of paper and place it under the pattern. Cut the first, second, and third right hand squares out of both sheets. Place this third page on top of the second page.

7. Place the fourth, uncut half sheet of paper behind the three cut out sheets, leaving four aligned tabs across the top of the book. Staple several times on the left side. You can also place glue along the left paper edges, and stack them together. The glued spine is very strong.

8. Cut a final half sheet of paper with no tabs and staple along the left side to form a cover.

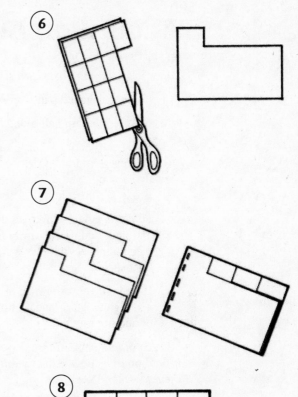

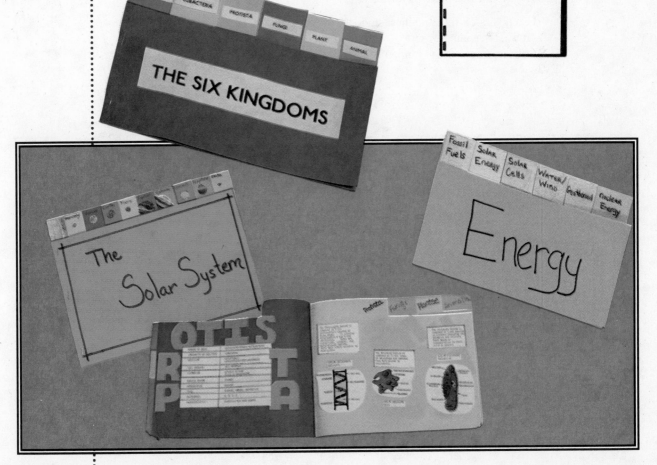

Accordion Book

NOTE: *Steps 1 and 2 should be done only if paper is too large to begin with.*

1. Fold the selected paper into *hamburgers*.

2. Cut the paper in half along the fold lines.

3. Fold each section of paper into *hamburgers*. However, fold one side one half inch shorter than the other side. This will form a tab that is one half inch long.

4. Fold this tab forward over the shorter side, and then fold it back away from the shorter piece of paper (in other words, fold it the opposite way).

5. Glue together to form an *accordion* by gluing a straight edge of one section into the *valley* of another section.

NOTE: *Stand the sections on end to form an accordion to help students visualize how to glue them together. (See illustration.)*

Always place the extra tab at the back of the book so you can add more pages later.

Use this book for timelines, student projects that grow, sequencing events or data, food chains and webs, systems of the human body, and more.

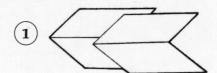

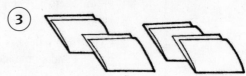

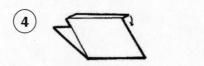

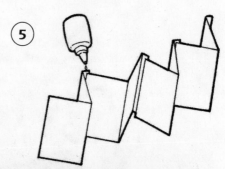

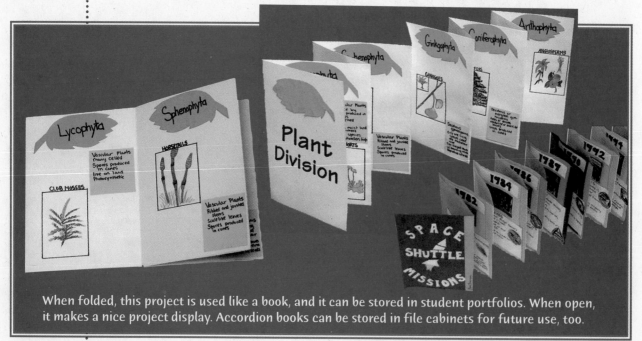

When folded, this project is used like a book, and it can be stored in student portfolios. When open, it makes a nice project display. Accordion books can be stored in file cabinets for future use, too.

Pop-Up Book

1. Fold a sheet of paper (8 1/2" × 11") in half like a *hamburger*.

2. Beginning at the fold, or *mountain* top, cut one or more tabs.

3. Fold the tabs back and forth several times until there is a good fold line formed.

4. Partially open the *hamburger* fold and push the tabs through to the inside.

5. With one small dot of glue, glue figures for the *pop-up book* to the front of each tab. Allow the glue to dry before going on to the next step.

6. Make a cover for the book by folding another sheet of paper in half like a *hamburger*. Place glue around the outside edges of the *pop-up book* and firmly press inside the *hamburger* cover.

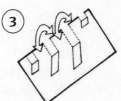

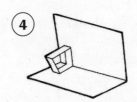

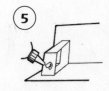

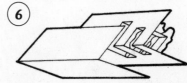

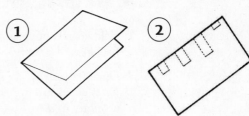

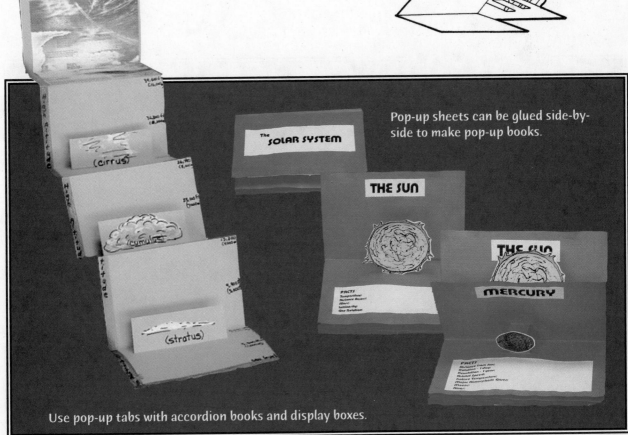

Pop-up sheets can be glued side-by-side to make pop-up books.

Use pop-up tabs with accordion books and display boxes.

Sentence-Strip Holder

1. Fold a sheet of paper (8 1/2" × 11") in half like a *hamburger.*

2. Open the *hamburger* and fold the two outer edges toward the *valley.* This forms a *shutter fold.*

3. Fold one of the inside edges of the shutter back to the outside fold. This fold forms a floppy "L."

4. Glue the floppy L-tab down to the base so that it forms a strong, straight L-tab.

5. Glue the other shutter side to the front of this L-tab. This forms a tent that is the backboard for the flashcards or student work to be displayed.

6. Fold the edge of the L-tab up one quarter to one half to form a lip that will keep the student work from slipping off the holder.

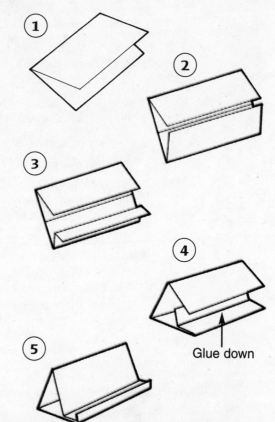

Glue down

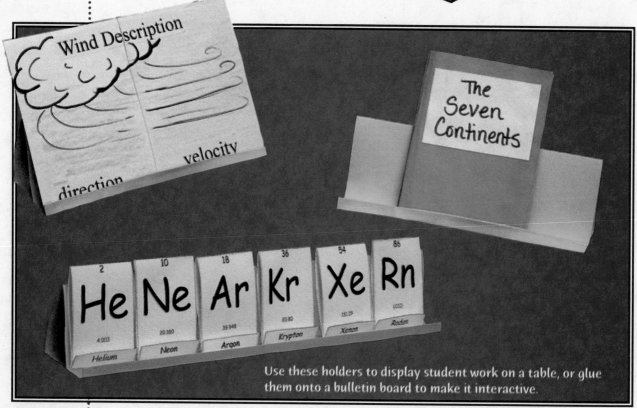

Use these holders to display student work on a table, or glue them onto a bulletin board to make it interactive.

Folding a Circle into Tenths

1. Fold a paper circle in half.

2. Fold the half circle so that one third is exposed and two thirds are covered.

3. Fold the one third (single thickness) backward to form a fold line.

4. Fold the two thirds section in half.

5. The half circle will be divided into fifths. When opened, the circle will be divided into tenths.

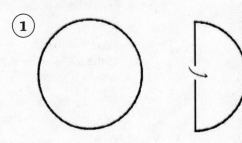

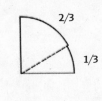

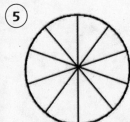

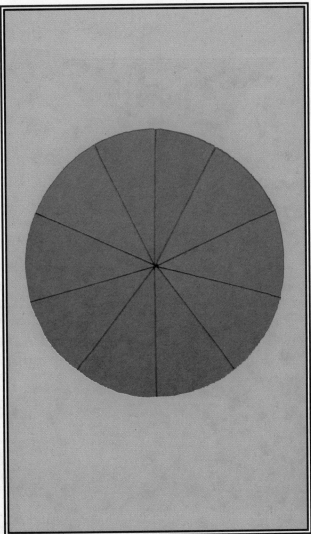

NOTE: *Paper squares and rectangles are folded into tenths the same way. Fold them so that one third is exposed and two thirds is covered. Continue with steps 3 and 4.*

Circle Graph

1. Cut out two circles using a pattern.

2. Fold one of the circles in half on each axis, forming fourths. Cut along one of the fold lines (the radius) to the middle of each circle. Flatten the circle.

3. Slip the two circles together along the cuts until they overlap completely.

4. Spin one of the circles while holding the other stationary. Estimate how much of each of the two (or you can add more) circles should be exposed to illustrate given percentages or fractional parts of data. Add circles to represent more than two percentages.

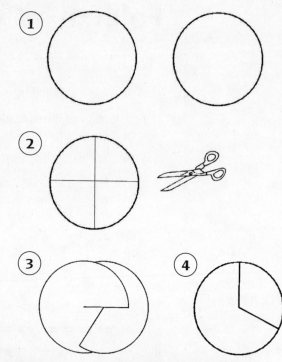

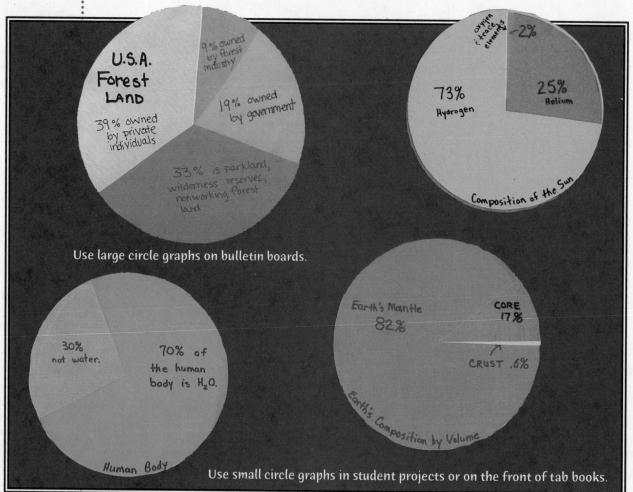

U.S.A. Forest Land

9% owned by forest industry

19% owned by government

39% owned by private individuals

33% is parkland, wilderness reserves, nonworking forest land

Composition of the Sun

73% Hydrogen

25% Helium

2%

oxygen & trace elements

Use large circle graphs on bulletin boards.

30% not water.

70% of the human body is H$_2$O.

Human Body

Earth's Mantle 82%

CORE 17%

CRUST .6%

Earth's Composition by Volume

Use small circle graphs in student projects or on the front of tab books.

Folded Table, Chart, or Graph

1. Fold the number of vertical columns needed to make the table or chart.

2. Fold the horizontal rows needed to make the table or chart.

3. Label the rows and columns.

Remember: Tables are organized along vertical and horizontal axes, while charts are organized along one axis, either horizontal or vertical.

Table

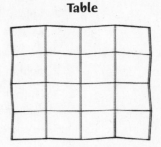

Chart

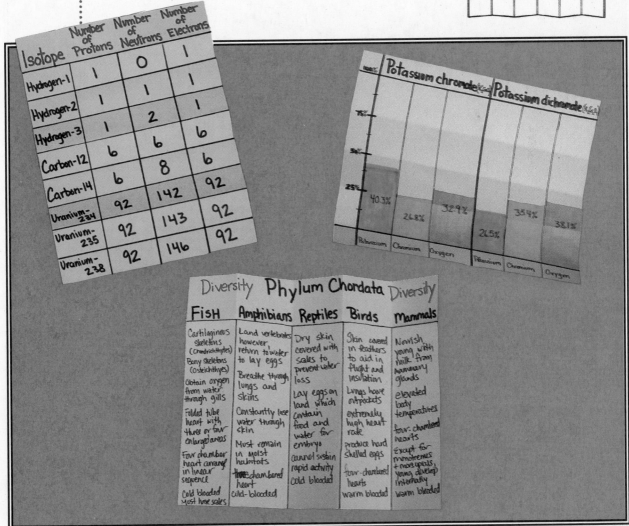

Concept-Map Book

1. Fold a sheet of paper along the long or short axis, leaving a two-inch tab uncovered along the top.

2. Fold in half or in thirds.

3. Unfold and cut along the two or three inside fold lines.

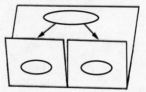

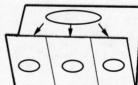

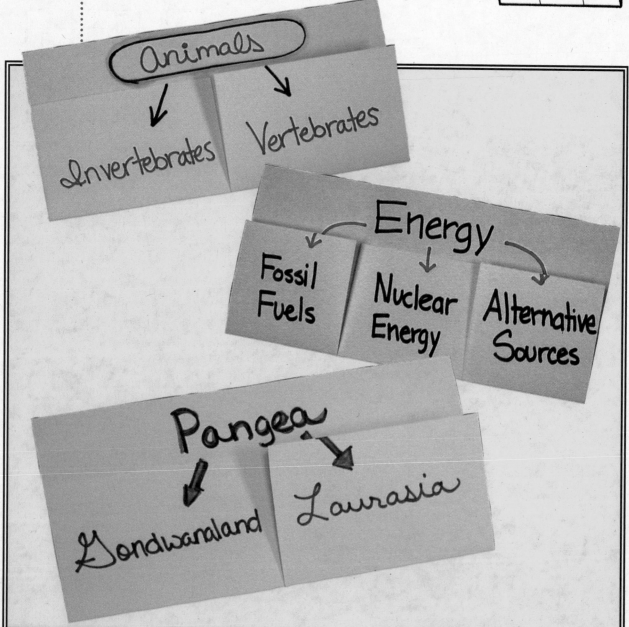

Vocabulary Book

1. Fold a sheet of notebook paper in half like a *hotdog*.

2. On one side, cut every third line. This usually results in ten tabs.

3. Label the tabs.

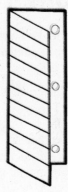

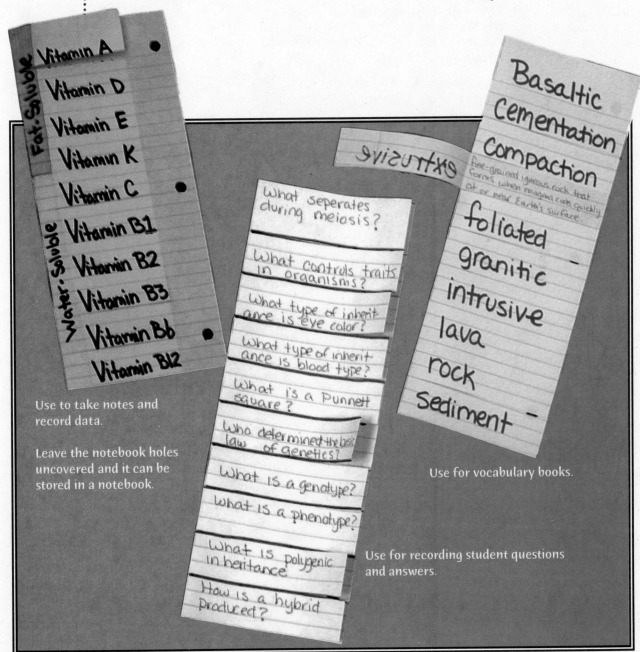

Fat-Soluble
Vitamin A
Vitamin D
Vitamin E
Vitamin K
Vitamin C

Water-Soluble
Vitamin B1
Vitamin B2
Vitamin B3
Vitamin B6
Vitamin B12

Use to take notes and record data.

Leave the notebook holes uncovered and it can be stored in a notebook.

What seperates during meiosis?

What controls traits in organisms?

What type of inheritance is eye color?

What type of inheritance is blood type?

What is a Punnett square?

Who determined the basic laws of genetics?

What is a genotype?

What is a phenotype?

What is polygenic inheritance?

How is a hybrid produced?

Extrusive

Basaltic
Cementation
Compaction
fine-grained igneous rock that forms when magma cools quickly at or near Earth's surface.
foliated
granitic
intrusive
lava
rock
sediment

Use for vocabulary books.

Use for recording student questions and answers.

Four-Door Diorama

1. Make a *four-door book* (see pg. 29) out of a *shutter fold*.

2. Fold the two inside corners back to the outer edges (*mountains*) of the *shutter fold*. This will result in two *tacos* that will make the *four-door book* look like it has a shirt collar. Do the same thing to the bottom of the *four-door book*. When finished, four small triangular *tacos* have been made.

3. Form a 90-degree angle and overlap the folded triangles to make a display case that doesn't use staples or glue. (It can be collapsed for storage.)

4. Or, as illustrated, cut off all four triangles, or *tacos*. Staple or glue the sides.

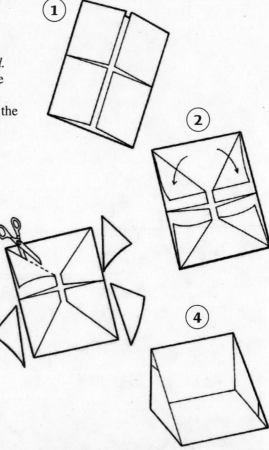

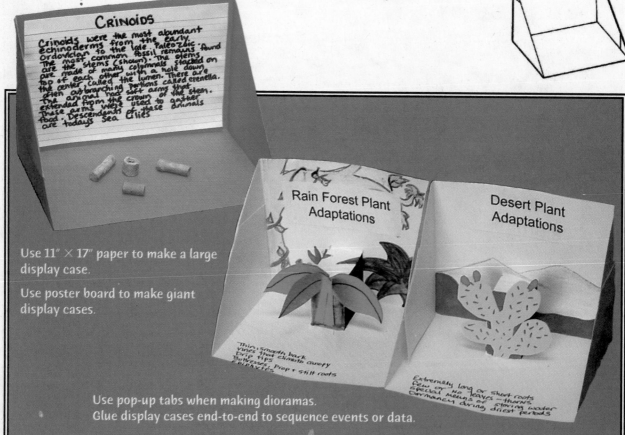

Use 11″ × 17″ paper to make a large display case.

Use poster board to make giant display cases.

Use pop-up tabs when making dioramas.
Glue display cases end-to-end to sequence events or data.

Picture-Frame Book

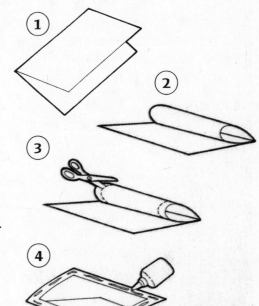

1. Fold a sheet of paper (8 1/2" × 11") in half like a *hamburger*.

2. Open the *hamburger* and gently roll one side of the *hamburger* toward the *valley*. Try not to crease the roll.

3. Cut a rectangle out of the middle of the rolled side of the paper leaving a half-inch border, forming a frame.

4. Fold another sheet of paper (8 1/2" × 11") in half like a *hamburger*. Apply glue to the inside border of the picture frame and place the folded, uncut sheet of paper inside.

Use this book to feature a person, place, or thing. Inside the picture frames, glue photographs, magazine pictures, computer-generated graphs, or have students sketch pictures. This book has three inside pages for writing and recording notes.

Display Case

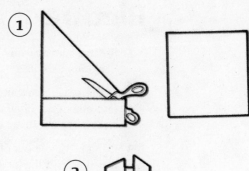

1. Make a *taco* fold and cut off the rectangular tab formed. This will result in a square.

2. Fold the square into a *shutter fold.*

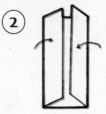

3. Unfold and fold the square into another *shutter fold* perpendicular to the direction of the first. This will form a small square at each of the four corners of the sheet of paper.

4. As illustrated, cut along two fold lines on opposite sides of the large square.

5. Collapse in and glue the cut tabs to form an open box.

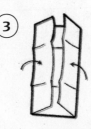
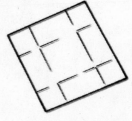

How to Make a Lid

Fold another open-sided box using a square of paper one half inch larger than the square used to make the first box. This will make a lid that fits snugly over the display box. *Example:* If the base is made out of an 8 1/2" paper square, then make the top out of a 9" square.

Cut a hole out of the lid and cover the opening with a cut piece of acetate used on overhead projectors. Heavy, clear plastic wrap or scraps from a laminating machine also will work. Secure the clear plastic sheet to the inside of the lid with glue or tape.

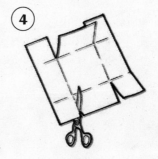

NOTE: *You can place polystyrene foam or quilt batting in the boxes to display insects. Glue the boxes onto a sheet of cardboard to make them strong enough to display rocks and minerals.*

Billboard Project

1. Fold all pieces of the same size of paper in half like *hamburgers*.

2. Place a line of glue at the top and bottom of one side of each folded billboard section and glue them edge-to-edge on a background paper or project board. If glued correctly, all doors will open from right to left.

3. Pictures, dates, words, etc., go on the front of each billboard section. When opened, writing or drawings can be seen on the inside left of each section. The base, or the part glued to the background, is perfect for more in-depth information or definitions.

Use for timelines or sequencing data, such as food chains, phases of the Moon, growth or development charts, and more.

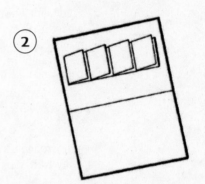

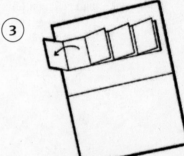

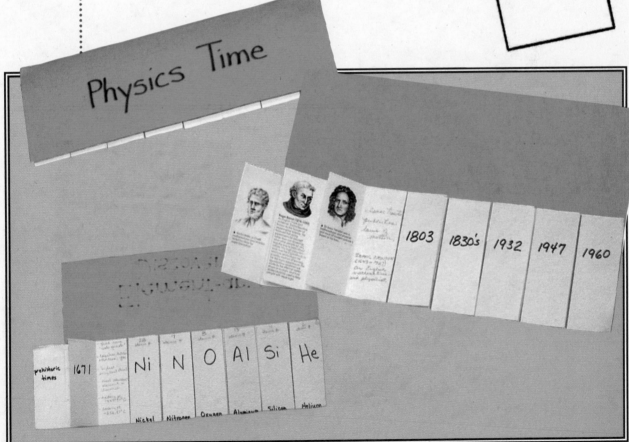

Project Board with Tabs

1. Draw a large illustration or a series of small illustrations or write on the front of one of the pieces of selected-size paper.

2. Pinch and slightly fold the paper at the point where a tab is desired on the illustrated project board. Cut into the paper on the fold. Cut straight in, then cut up to form an "L." When the paper is unfolded, it will form a tab with an illustration on the front.

3. After all tabs have been cut, glue this front sheet onto a second piece of paper. Place glue around all four edges and in the middle, away from tabs.

Write or draw under the tabs. If the project is made as a bulletin board using butcher paper, quarter and half-sheets of paper can be glued under the tabs.

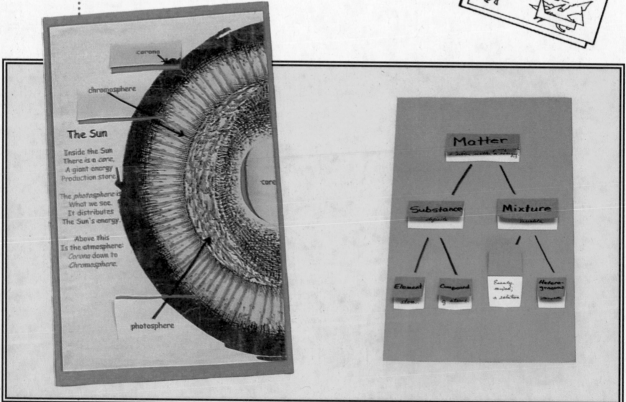

Science Activities Using Foldables

The following pages are divided into these categories:

- *Physical Science/Physics*
- *Astronomy*
- *Earth Science*
- *Life Science/Biology*

For your convenience, a table of contents precedes each category. Under each topic you will find a list of activities you can use to augment your lesson plan with Foldables. Activities are listed alphabetically according to the skill that students will practice. The suggested number of Foldable parts is also included.

Foldables for Physical Science/Physics

The following science topics are covered in this section:

Acid, Base, Salt

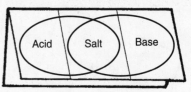

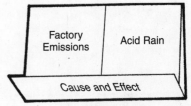

Three-tab Venn diagram

Skill	Activity Suggestion	Foldable Parts
chart	foods as acid, neutral (pure water is close to neutral), or base	3
compare and contrast	acids and bases	2
	differentiate between strength and concentration	2
define	acid, base, neutral, salt	4
	salts formed by the neutralization of an acid and base	1
diagram	a color-coded pH scale; 0–14	any number
explain	procedures for neutralizing things that are acidic	1
	buffers and their importance (they maintain constant pH when acids or bases are added)	1
	why many water spots and deposits can be cleaned with vinegar	1
	observe what happens to a chicken bone in vinegar	1
	acid and nonacid soils and how they are formed	2
graph	pH levels of different foods	any number
investigate	experiments with litmus paper indicators	any number
	common household items that are bases, such as toothpaste, ammonia, and baking soda	any number
list	plants that need acidic soil and plants that need alkaline soil	2
	examples of substances that are acidic, neutral, and basic	3
make a Venn diagram	of common properties of acids and bases. For example: 1) many can conduct electricity, 2) acids react with bases to form neutral salt and water, called neutralization, and 3) acids and bases change the color of indicators.	3
	of acid, base, and salt	3
question	create a "know?-like to know?-learned?" about acids, bases, salts	3
research	the positive and negative effects of the corrosiveness of acids	2
	how to treat insect stings that are acidic and those that are basic	2
	methods for making natural acid and base indicators and homemade litmus paper. For example: red cabbage and water	2
	the halogen group of elements, or salt formers	any number
	the "who, what, when, where" of Soren Sorensen	4
show cause and effect	of rainwater becoming more acidic	1
	of tooth decay as it relates to acids and bases	1
	of bases reacting with fats to form items such as soaps	1

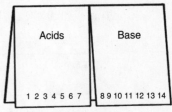

Two-tab match book

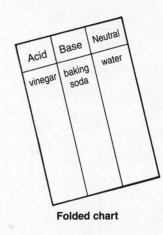

Folded chart

Two-tab book

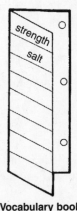

Vocabulary book

Atoms and Molecules

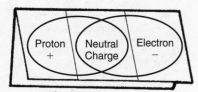

Layered book

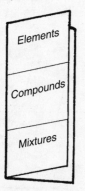

Three-tab Venn diagram

Elements

Compounds

Mixtures

Three-tab book

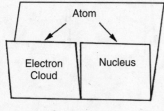

Concept map

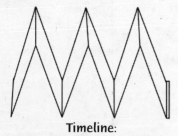

Timeline:
History of Atomic Model

Skill	Activity Suggestion	Foldable Parts
compare and contrast	an atom of iron and a molecule of water	2
	adhesion and cohesion	2
	isotopes and radioactive isotopes	2
	compounds and atoms	2
	elements, compounds, and mixtures	3
define	density (the mass of matter per unit volume)	1
	compound formulas and give examples; include what elements are present and how many atoms of each element are in the compounds	any number
describe	parts of an atom, including electrons, protons, and neutrons	3
discuss	the statement "All atoms are in constant motion."	1
explain	that all matter is made of atoms	1
	the statement "Compounds can be made of only one atom or made up of numerous atoms."	1
	the statement "An electron with a proton equals a neutral charge."	1
	how atoms differ in their number of electrons, protons, and neutrons	any number
	how heating and cooling matter affects molecular movement	1
identify	parts of a nucleus, including protons and neutrons	2
illustrate	electron cloud and nucleus	2
	molecular movement in solids, liquids, and gases	3
	the attraction of like molecules (cohesion)	any number
	the attraction of different molecules (adhesion)	any number
investigate	how density is affected by heating and cooling	2
	electrons, including information on their charge, amount of energy, and mass	any number
	protons, including information on their charge, amount of energy, and mass	any number
	neutrons and neutrinos	2
make a Venn diagram	labeled *protons, neutrons,* and *both* about atomic number and mass number	3
question	create a "know?-like to know?-learned?" about atoms and compounds	3
research	how protons and neutrons can be broken down into quarks (which are up, down, strange, charmed, top, and bottom)	6
	electrons and energy levels	any number
	the history of the periodic table of elements	1
	the "who, what, when, where" of any of the following people: Lorenzo Avogadro, William Cookes, Peter Joseph William Debyl, Werner Karl Heisenberg, Robert Hofstadler	4
sequence	the development of the atomic model, including Democritus, Lavoisier, John Dalton, William Crookes, J.J. Thompson, Ernest Rutherford, James Chadwick, and Niels Bohr	any number
show cause and effect	of expansion and contraction	2

Carbon Cemistry

Skill	Activity Suggestion	Foldable Parts
compare and contrast	organic and inorganic carbon compounds	2
	saturated hydrocarbons (single bonds between carbon atoms) and unsaturated hydrocarbons (multiple bonds)	2
	monomers and polymers	2
describe	biological compounds, including carbohydrates, lipids, proteins, and nucleic acids	4
examine	the structures of some organic compounds	any number
explain	the statement "Petroleum is a mixture of thousands of carbon compounds."	1
graph	organic carbon compounds	any number)
illustrate	how carbon atoms bond, including chains, branched chains, and rings	3
investigate	aromatic compounds (benzine rings) and alchohols and acids (OH and COOH groups)	2
list	examples of hydrocarbons, which are compounds made of hydrogen and carbon	any number
question	create a "know?-like to know?-learned?" about organic compounds	3
research	biological organic compounds, including lipids, carbohydrates, proteins, and nucleic acids	4
	the "who, what, when, where" of any of the following people: Friedrich Wohler, William Henry Perkin, Paul John Flory	4

Three-tab book

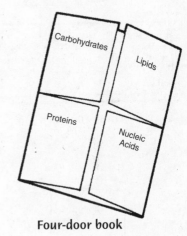

Four-door book

Chemical Bonds and Reactions

Skill	Activity Suggestion	Foldable Parts
compare and contrast	covalent bonding and ionic bonding	2
	nonpolar and polar covalent bonds	2
describe	covalent, ionic, and metallic bonding	3
diagram	a concept map that explains ions and their gain and loss of electrons	2
	reactants and products	2
explain	the statement "All chemical reactions involve the formation or destruction of bonds between atoms."	1
	how chemical reactions can be sped up with catalysts and slowed down by inhibitors	2
	the cause and effect of chemical reaction rates that are influenced by temperature, concentration, and particle size	3
investigate	synthesis reactions, including single and double displacement reactions	2
	decomposition reactions, including exergonic and endergonic reactions	2
list	examples of endothermic and exothermic reactions	2
make a Venn diagram	labeled *endothermic, exothermic,* and *both*	3
question	create a "know?-like to know?-learned?" about chemical bonds	3
	create a "know?-like to know?-learned?" about chemical reactions	3
research	positive and negative effects of chemical reactions	2
	the "who, what, when, where" of Gilbert Newton Lewis	4

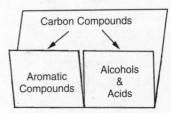

Concept-map book

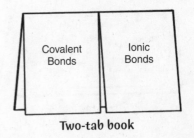

Two-tab book

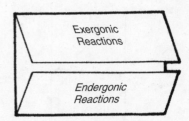

Shutter-fold book

Electricity

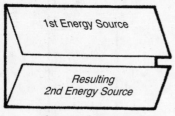

Shutter-fold book

1st Energy Source

Resulting
2nd Energy Source

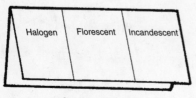

Three-tab book

Halogen | Florescent | Incandescent

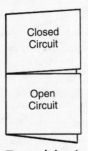

Two-tab book

Closed Circuit

Open Circuit

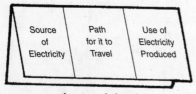

Three-tab book

Source of Electricity | Path for it to Travel | Use of Electricity Produced

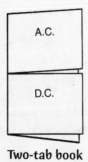

Two-tab book

A.C.

D.C.

Skill	Activity Suggestion	Foldable Parts
compare and contrast	halogen, fluorescent, and incandescent bulbs	3
	electrostatic attraction and repulsion	2
	static electricity and electric current	2
	a closed circuit and an open circuit	2
	a series circuit and a parallel circuit	2
	wet cell and dry cell	2
	direct current and alternating current	2
define	static electricity (which is an accumultion of excess electric charge)	1
	volt, ampere, ohm, watt, watt-hour, kilowatt-hour	6
describe	how electric current is generated by an energy source such as oil, gas, coal, or nuclear power	any number
	lightning as an electric spark produced by static electricity	1
	an electric current as the flow of negatively charged electrons	1
diagram	a simple electric circuit, including a voltage source, a path for current to travel, and something that uses the electric energy carried by the current	3
	parts of a lightbulb	any number
	the hours that specific electric appliances are in use during a given time (use a graph)	any number
explain	how electric energy can be transferred as other kinds of energy such as heat, light, sound and kinetic energy	4
	the uses of conductors and insulators	2
	how an electromagnet in an electric motor converts electrical energy to mechanical energy	1
identify	the forms of energy that can be transformed into electrical energy, including chemical, mechanical, light, heat, fossil fuels, nuclear, and others	any number
investigate	causes of static electricity	any number
make a timeline	for the history of electricity	any number
make a Venn diagram	labeled with *conductors, insulators,* and *semiconductors*	3
question	create a "know?-like to know?-learned?" about electricity	3
research	two kinds of electric charges (positive and negative)	2
	the factors that influence how much electrical energy is used, including the length of time energy is used, and the rate at which the energy is used	any number
	turbines and generators	2
	the purpose of generators, including information on how they produce electrical energy from mechanical energy	1
	the generation of electricity with water, wind, and solar sources	3
	the "what, when, where, why" of Ohm's law	4
	the "who, what, when, where" of any of the following people: Benjamin Franklin, Alessandro Volta, John Ambrose Fleming	4
show cause and effect	of a complete and an incomplete circuit	2
write	an electricity safety manual	1

Electromagnetic Waves

Skill	Activity Suggestion	Foldable Parts
compare and contrast	waves that need matter to transfer energy and those that do not need matter to transfer energy	2
	invisible and visible electromagnetic waves	2
	electromagnetic waves with long wavelengths and those with short wavelengths	2
	electromagnetic and particle radiation	2
define	electromagnetic waves	1
	wavelength, frequency, and cycle	3
describe	what happens to ultraviolet rays entering Earth's atmosphere (some are absorbed by the ozone layer and some are not)	2
	X rays and their medical uses (for example, X rays are absorbed by bone and diseased cell tissue)	1
diagram	the electromagnetic wave spectrum, including radio waves, microwaves, infrared waves, visible light, ultraviolet rays, X rays, and gamma rays	7
	how electromagnetic waves vibrate (both electric field and magnetic field vibrations)	1
	the location of the ozone layer in Earth's atmosphere	1
explain	what happens when electromagnetic waves hit a solid, liquid, or gas	3
investigate	how a microwave oven works	any number
make a timeline	for the history of the electromagnetic spectrum	any number
make a Venn diagram	labeled *electric energy, magnetic energy,* and *both* for the statement "Electromagnetic radiation consists of electric energy and magnetic energy"	3
	labeled *AM waves, FM waves,* and *both* (television signals are both)	3
question	create a "know?-like to know?-learned?" about electromagnetic radiation	3
research	cycle, kilocycle, and megacycle	3
	how infrared waves are used by humans, insects, and other animals	3
	X rays, including medicine and industry uses	any number
	the harmful effects and beneficial uses of gamma rays	2
	the statement "All types of electromagnetic radiation travel through space at the same speed."	1
	the "who, what, when, where" for any of the following people: Joseph Henry, Robert Wilhelm Bunsen, James Clerk Maxwell, Heinrich Rudolph Hertz	4

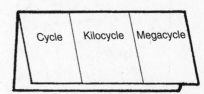

Layered book
(4 sheets of paper)

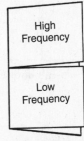

Two-tab book

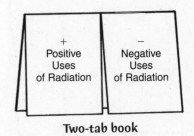

Three-tab book

Two-tab book

Bound-book journal

Energy

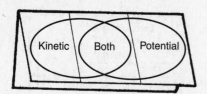

Three-tab Venn diagram

Kinetic | Both | Potential

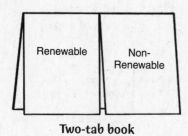

Renewable | Non-Renewable

Two-tab book

Law of Conservation of Mass and Energy

Half book

Source	Cause	Effect
Sun	Nuclear Reaction	Light Heat
—	—	—
—	—	—

Folded table

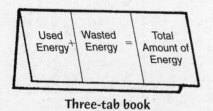

Used Energy + Wasted Energy = Total Amount of Energy

Three-tab book

Skill	Activity Suggestion	Foldable Parts
compare and contrast	kinds of energy, including kinetic and potential energy	2
	renewable and nonrenewable energy sources	2
	the cost of using renewable and nonrenewable fuels	2
	energy efficient and inefficient tools and machines	2
debate	the statement "Every change in the universe represents the change of energy from one form into another."	2
	why energy cannot be created or destroyed but can be transferred from one piece of matter to another	2
describe	transformation of energy	1
diagram	energy being changed from one form to another	any number
discuss	the statement "Energy is usually wasted as heat energy."	1
	the statement "No engine functions at 100 percent efficiency or transforms all its energy into useful work."	1
explain	how kinetic energy can become potential energy and potential can become kinetic	2
	how useful energy and wasted energy always add up to exactly the total amount of energy used	1
identify	radiant energy, including light rays, radio waves, infrared rays, ultraviolet rays, cosmic waves, radiant heat waves, and more	any number
investigate	how energy is involved when physical or chemical changes occur	any number
list	forms of energy, including mechanical, thermal, electrical, wave, chemical, nuclear, and others	any number
	natural sources of energy, including wood, sunlight, wind, waves, tides, and others	any number
	nuclear sources of energy or fuels, including uranium and plutonium	any number
	causes and effects of different energy transformations (for example, the Sun has energy through nuclear reactions which cause light, heat, photosynthesis, and more)	any number
question	create a "know?-like to know?-learned?" about energy	3
research	different kinds of wave energy	any number
	energy-efficient appliances and see if there is empirical data to back up such claims	any number
	the "who, what, when, where" of any of the following people: Gustave Gaspard Coriolis, James Prescott Joule, Hermann Ludwig von Helmholtz, Albert Einstein	4

Fluids

Skill	Activity Suggestion	Foldable Parts
compare and contrast	static fluids and fluids in motion	2
	the three branches of fluid mechanics: fluid statistics (the balance between gravity and pressure in fluids at rest), external fluid mechanics (forces acting on a stationary object in a moving fluid, including aerodynamics and hydrodynamics), and internal fluid mechanics (fluid flowing through containers or pipes)	3
	pressure created by liquids and pressure created by gases	2
define	types of fluid motion, including steady flow, unsteady flow, and turbulent flow	3
describe	gases and liquids as fluids	2
explain	what happens to gases when there is a change in pressure, temperature, or volume	3
	Boyle's law, Gay-Lussac's law, and Avogadro's law	3
investigate	the properties of fluids through experimentation	any number
make a timeline	for key events in our understanding of fluids	any number
question	create a "know?-like to know?-learned?" about fluids	3
research	fluid mechanics and how this science is used	2
	the properties of fluids, including Archimdedes' Principle, Pascal's Principle, and Bernoulli's Principle	3
	the universal law of gases (Boyle's law, Charles's law, and Avogadro's law combined explain how the pressure, temperature, volume, and the number of particles in a container of gas are related)	any number
	why Charles's law is called Gay-Lussac's law	1
	the "who, what, when, where" of any of the following people: Archimedes, Evangelista Torricelli, Blaise Pascal, Robert Boyle, Daniel Bernouli, Joseph Louis Gay-Lussac	4

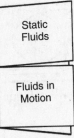

Two-tab book

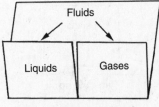

Concept-map book

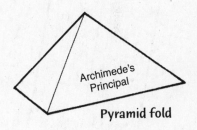

Pyramid fold

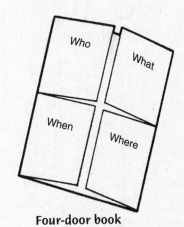

Four-door book

layered book
(2 sheets of paper)

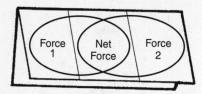

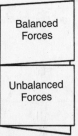

Three-tab book

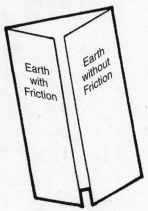

Balanced Forces

Unbalanced Forces

Two-tab book

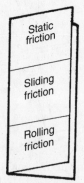

Earth with Friction

Earth without Friction

Shutter-fold book

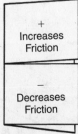

Static friction

Sliding friction

Rolling friction

Three-tab book

+
Increases Friction

–
Decreases Friction

Two-tab book

Forces

Skill	Activity Suggestion	Foldable Parts
compare and contrast	balanced and unbalanced forces	2
define	a force as a push or pull that one object exerts on another	2
	net force as resultant force	2
describe	how force, mass, and acceleration are related	3
	forces acting on a moving car, a person running, and a bridge	3
design	an activity that demonstrates centripetal force	any number
diagram	examples of balanced and unbalanced forces	2
explain	how forces can change motion	1
	how Newton's 2nd and 3rd laws of motion relate to forces	2
make a Venn diagram	labeled with *force one*, *net force*, and *force two*	3
question	create a "know?-like to know?-learned?" about forces	3
research	forces that are and are not felt	2

Friction

Skill	Activity Suggestion	Foldable Parts
compare and contrast	a world with and without friction	2
demonstrate	how friction works to make things stop moving while producing heat	any number
describe	three different types of friction (static, sliding, and rolling)	3
design an experiment	to prove that the greater the force pressing objects together, the greater the friction	any number
explain	causes of friction, including a description of how all surfaces have bumps and hollows, or microwelds, and when they come in contact with other objects, their textured surfaces catch	any number
	how friction makes work harder because more force is needed to overcome it	1
investigate	whether rough surfaces produce more friction than smooth	2
	ways to increase and decrease friction	2
list	the positive and negative effect of friction as a force in the world	2
make a timeline	to show the development of technology to overcome or lessen friction	any number
question	create a "know?-like to know?-learned?" about friction	3
	how lubricants reduce friction, including oil, grease, glycerine, soap, wax, graphite	6
research	conditions that might affect friction, including texture of surfaces, nature of materials, and force pressing surfaces together	3
	the beneficial and harmful effects of friction	2
	the impact of using water as an industrial lubricant	1
show cause and effect	of increasing friction to increase safety	any number
write	about "frictional" encounters during an average day	any number

Gravity

Skill	Activity Suggestion	Foldable Parts
compare and contrast	the force of gravity on Earth and the force of gravity on the Moon (the Moon's gravity is 1/6th that of Earth's)	2
	weight and mass	2
describe	the effect of gravity on vertical and horizontal motion	2
design an experiment	to show if objects with the same shape and same mass take the same time to fall	any number
	to show the rates at which objects of different shapes and masses fall	any number
discuss	the statement "Mass is the same on Earth as on the Moon, but weight is not."	any number
explain	the law of universal gravitation, which is that the force of gravity between two objects is affected by the amount of matter in objects and the distance between the objects	2
investigate	the center of gravity of several objects	any number
	the effect of mass on gravitational pull	any number
	the effect of distance on gravitational pull	any number
	how Earth's gravity affects the Moon	2
	air resistance, terminal speed, and free fall	3
list	things that gravity affects on Earth, including keeping objects earthbound, water seeking lowest point, objects falling, moving groundwater, and causing erosion	any number
question	create a "know?-like to know?-learned?" about gravity	3
relate	what would happen to the Universe without gravity, including how gravity holds gases within stars and keeps on objects in orbit	any number
research	the "who, what, when, where" of Sir Isaac Newton	4

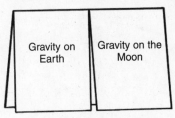

Two-tab book (horizontal)

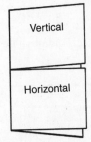

Two-tab book (vertical)

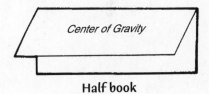

Half book

Inertia

Skill	Activity Suggestion	Foldable Parts
compare and contrast	inertia and gravity	2
define	inertia, including that 1) objects at rest tend to stay at rest, and 2) objects moving tend to continue moving	2
	inertia as a property of matter and mass as a measure of inertia	1
describe	how the combined effects of gravity and inertia keep the Moon in orbit around Earth, and Earth in orbit around the Sun	2
outline	Sir Isaac Newton's first law of motion	any number
question	create a "know?-like to know?-learned?" about inertia	3
research	the reasons for the extra expense of adding headrests and seat belts to cars	any number
	gyroscopic inertia and use it to explain Earth's rotation around an imaginary axis while moving through space	1

Four-door book

Light

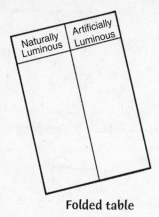

Folded table

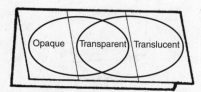

Three-tab Venn diagram

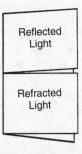

Two-tab book

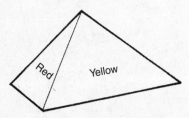

Pyramid fold

Visible Light Spectrum
Red
Orange
Yellow
Green
Blue
Indigo
Violet

Layered book
(4 sheets of paper)

Skill	Activity Suggestion	Foldable Parts
compare and contrast	objects that are luminous and objects that are illuminated	2
	opaque, translucent, and transparent	3
	light reflecting off both rough and smooth surfaces	2
	reflected light and refracted light	2
	colors, including primary pigment colors and primary light colors	4
	the human eye and a camera	2
define	luminous	1
describe	things that are naturally luminous, such as the Sun, stars, and fire, and things that are artificially luminous, such as lightbulbs and lasers	2
design an experiment	to show that light rays travel in a straight line	any number
	with a prism	any number
diagram	shadows, including umbra and penumbra	any number
	a spectrum, including red, orange, yellow, green, blue, indigo, and violet	7
	a color wheel showing primary and secondary colors	any number
	an incident ray, angle of incidence, and angle of reflection	3
investigate	different ways in which light is produced, such as incandescent bulbs, fluorescent bulbs, neon lights, and lasers	4
	light as it relates to vision	1
make a Venn diagram	labeled *opaque, transparent,* and *translucent*	3
observe	direct, semi-direct, and indirect lighting	3
question	create a "know?-like to know?-learned?" about light	3
research	why light has been said to be the fastest thing known and determine if this is still true	1
	natural and human-made prisms	2
	fact and lore of rainbows	2
	fact and lore of mirages	2
	the "who, what, when, where" of any of the following people: Isaac Newton, Christian Huygens, Claus Roemer, Thomas Young, Albert Abraham Michelson, Albert Einstein	4
	lunar and solar eclipses as shadows	2
	how sunlight is absorbed and reflected	2
	measurement of long distances using the light-year and parsec	1

Magnetism

Skill	Activity Suggestion	Foldable Parts
compare and contrast	magnetic and nonmagnetic matter	2
	natural magnets and commercially produced magnets	2
design an experiment	using magnets named by their shape, including bar, ring, horseshoe, U-shaped, disc, and block	any number
	to show how like poles repel	any number
	to show how opposite poles attract	any number
	to show matter that a magnetic force can pass through, including wood, plastic, glass, and others	any number
	to show that a magnet can be used to magnetize something metal	any number
diagram	geologic formations of the mineral magnetite on a map	any number
	a bar magnet placed in iron fillings	1
explain	how a magnet works, including how a force pulls together a magnet and objects made out of iron or steel	1
	force of magnetism, including attraction and repulsion	2
	magnetic field and lines of force	2
graph	30 objects as either magnetic or nonmagnetic	2
identify	magnetic and nonmagnetic matter	2
	poles of different-shaped magnets, including both north and south poles	2
investigate	the properties of magnetic materials, including iron, steel, cobalt, and nickel	any number
	lodestone rocks, including geographic location, physical characteristics, discovery, and early uses	any number
list	the steps for magnetizing a piece of metal	any number
make a timeline	from the discovery of magnetite to the use of magnets in technology	any number
question	create a "know?-like to know?-learned?" about magnets	3
research	the magnetic lines of force of Earth and draw them	any number
	the "who, what, when, where" of any of the following people: William Gilbert, Hans Oersted, Andre Ampere, Michael Faraday, Joseph Henry, Nikola Tesla	4

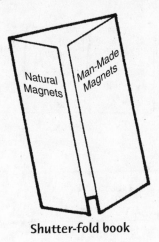

Shutter-fold book

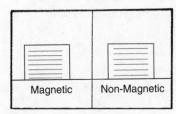

Pocket book

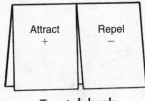

Two-tab book

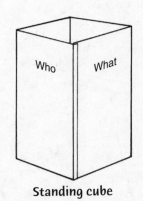

Standing cube

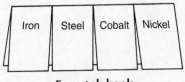

Four-tab book

Matter

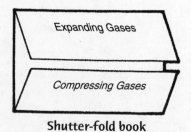

Two-tab book

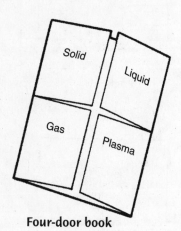

Shutter-fold book

Skill	Activity Suggestion	Foldable Parts
compare and contrast	ancient Greek and modern theories of what composed the universe (fire, water, land, and air versus matter and energy)	2
	matter and antimatter	2
define	matter, including that it occupies space and has weight	1
	gases and liquids as fluids	2
describe	characteristics of solids, including definite size and a definite shape	2
	characteristics of liquids, including definite size but not definite shape	2
	characteristics of gases, which have neither a definite size nor a definite shape	2
	the motion of particles in solids, liquids, and gases	
	how gases can be expanded and compressed	2
design an experiment	to prove the statement "Two pieces of matter can't occupy the same space at the same time."	any number
discuss	the statement "Everything in the known world is either matter or energy."	1
explain	how matter can be changed by adding or deleting heat	2
identify	types of matter, including that 1) some things are made of only one type of atom called an element, and 2) some are made of more than one kind of atom called a compound	2
investigate	matter and energy	2
list	examples of matter, including organic and inorganic	2
	states of matter, including solid, liquid, gas, and plasma	4
	examples of common solids, liquids, and gases	3
make a Venn diagram	labeled *organic, inorganic,* and *both*	3
question	create a "know?-like to know?-learned?" about matter	3
research	what "elements" the ancient Greeks thought composed the universe, including fire, water, land, and air	4
	the "who, what, when, where" of any of the following people: John Dalton and Antoine Laurent Lavoisier	4

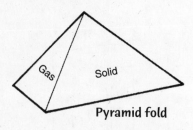

Four-door book

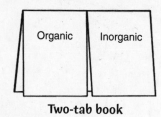

Pyramid fold

Physical and Chemical Properties

Skill	Activity Suggestion	Foldable Parts
discuss	chemical properties of matter, including reactive and unreactive	2
investigate	properties of matter, including physical and chemical properties	2
list	examples of matter changes, including physical and chemical changes	2
make a table	to document the physical properties of different pieces of matter, including any of the following properties: color, taste, odor, weight, hardness, luster, elasticity, melting and boiling temperatures, dissolvability, acidity, ability to conduct heat and electricity, magnetic or nonmagnetic, buoyancy, and others	any number
observe	physical properties of selected matter using the five senses	5
question	create a "know?-like to know?-learned?" about properties of matter	3

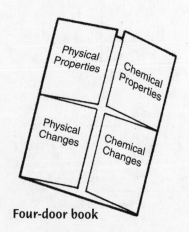

Four-door book

Motion and Speed

Skill	Activity Suggestion	Foldable Parts
compare and contrast	rectilinear motion (objects move in straight lines) and curvilinear motion (objects move along a curved path)	2
	distance and displacement	2
debate	the statement "Everything in the universe is in motion."	2
define	momentum	1
describe	motion using the terms *displacement, velocity,* and *acceleration*	3
	how velocity and speed differ	2
	how objects obtain momentum and kinetic energy from forces acting on them for a period of time	any number
	how some athletes apply force to a ball for the longest time possible to get it to have greater momentum and kinetic energy	any number
design an experiment	to show that a free-falling object has a constant acceleration of 9.8 m/s^2	any number
discuss	how motion occurs when an object changes its position in space	1
explain	how your body is moving even as you sit or lie stationary	1
	why kinetic energy is often called the "energy of motion"	1
graph	distance-time, including distance on the vertical axis and time on the horizontal axis	any number
question	create a "know?-like to know?-learned?" about motion	3
research	the three laws of motion	3
	apparent motion	1
	the "who, what, when, where" of Sir Isaac Newton	4

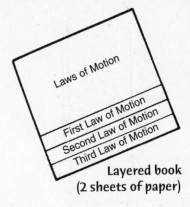

Layered book
(2 sheets of paper)

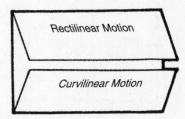

Shutter-fold book

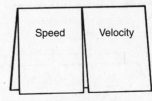

Two-tab book

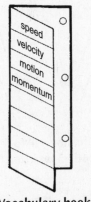

Vocabulary book

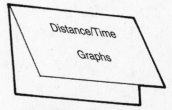

Half book with graphs

Mirrors and Lenses

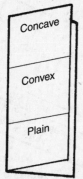

Three-tab book

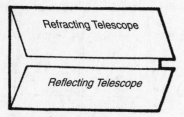

Two-tab book

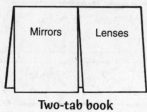

Shutter-fold book

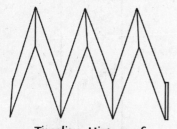

Timeline: History of Optical Instruments

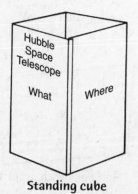

Standing cube

Skill	Activity Suggestion	Foldable Parts
compare and contrast	real and virtual images	2
	mirrors and lenses	2
	refracting and reflecting telescopes	2
debate	the use of two-way mirrors in public places	2
	the cost of placing a telescope in space	2
describe	how an image looks if viewed in each type of mirror	3
diagram	plane, concave, and convex mirrors	3
	a mirror image	1
	how a concave mirror works	any number
	how a convex mirror works	any number
	the human eye	any number
	how a microscope uses two convex lenses	any number
explain	the sequence of events involved in seeing the reflection of yourself in mirror	any number
	how concave and convex lenses refract light to form images	1
	the sequence of events leading to the invention of the telescope	any number
make a table	of information on the images formed by concave and convex mirrors and lenses	any number
make a timeline	on the history of mirrors and lenses	any number
	on the history of optical instruments, including telescopes, microscopes, and cameras	any number
observe	how reflective surfaces with different textures do or do not scatter light	2
question	create a "know?-like to know?-learned?" about mirrors and lenses	3
research	how a periscope works	1
	the "what, where, when, why" of the Hubble Space Telescope	4
	the "who, what, when, where" of any of the following people: Han Lippershey, Christiaan Huygens, Jean Augustin Fresnel, Jean Bernard Leon Foucault, Alvan Graham Clark, George Ellery Hale	4
show cause and effect	of vision correction, including concave and convex eyeglass lenses	2

Radioactivity

Skill	Activity Suggestion	Foldable Parts
compare and contrast	stable and unstable nuclei	2
	alpha, beta, and gamma radiation	3
	nuclear fission and nuclear fusion	2
define	half-life as the amount of time it takes for half of the atoms in a radioactive sample to decay	1
describe	three common types of radiation emitted from a decaying nucleus, including alpha particles, beta particles, and gamma rays	3
diagram	the structure of an atom and its nucleus	any number
	a cross-section of the Sun and explain how nuclear fusion occurs	any number
explain	radioactivity	1
	how a chain reaction occurs	1
investigate	uses of radioactive carbon (carbon-14) and radioactive uranium isotopes for calculating the ages of objects that contain these substances	2
	background radiation	1
make a table	to illustrate half-life	any number
make a timeline	on the discovery of radioactivity	any number
outline	radioactive dating of a sample	any number
question	create a "know?-like to know?-learned?" about radioactivity	3
research	the four fundamental forces of nature, including strong force, electromagnetic force, weak force, and weakest force (gravity)	4
	cosmic rays	
	methods for detecting radioactivity, including cloud chamber, bubble chamber, electroscope, and Geiger counter	4
	the "who, what, when, where" of any of the following people: Antoine Henri Bacquerel, Marie and Pierre Curie, Frederick Soddy, Otto Hahn, Hans Wilhelm Geiger, James Chadwick, Julius Robert Oppenheimer, Donald Arthur Glaser	4
show cause and effect	of nuclear reactions and cancer treatment	2
write	a safety manual for the use of radioactive materials	any number

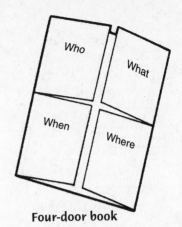

Four-door book

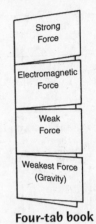

Four-tab book

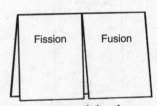

Two-tab book

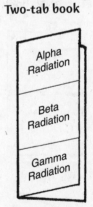

Three-tab book

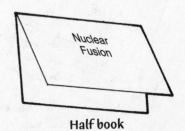

Half book

Physical Science/Physics **61**

Solutions

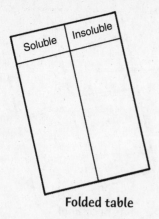

Folded table

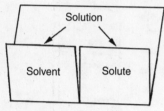

Concept-map book

Three-tab book

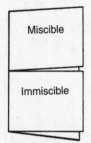

Two-tab book

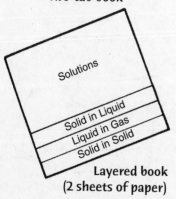

**Layered book
(2 sheets of paper)**

Skill	Activity Suggestion	Foldable Parts
compare and contrast	diluted, concentrated, and saturated solutions	3
define	solution as a mixture that has the same color, density, and composition throughout	1
	a solution as a homogeneous mixture in which the particles are distributed evenly at the molecular or ionic level	1
demonstrate	how crystal size, temperature, and the act of stirring affects solubility of a solid in a liquid	3
describe	the three phases of solutions, including solid, liquid, and gas	3
	saturated, unsaturated, and supersaturated solutions	3
	solutions that are miscible and immiscible	2
explain	chemical reactions that take place in a solution (for example, digestion)	any number
investigate	how a solute dissolves in a solvent	1
	the law of conservation of matter	1
list	examples of solutions encountered in a given amount of time	any number
	solutions that do and do not dissolve in water	2
	substances that are soluble or insoluble in water	2
	examples of solid-solid, solid-liquid, liquid-liquid, liquid-gas, and gas-gas solutions	5
make a concept map	for a solution composed of solvents and solutes	2
measure	solubility of gases in liquids	any number
outline	how a solid dissolves in a liquid	3
question	create a "know?-like to know?-learned?" about solutions	3
research	ways to make solids dissolve faster in liquids, including stirring, powdering, and heating the liquid	3
	the "who, what, when, where" of Svante Arrhenius	4

Sound

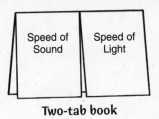

Two-tab book

Skill	Activity Suggestion	Foldable Parts
compare and contrast	pitch and frequency	2
	sound moving through warm air and cold air	2
	sound movement through liquids and gases	2
	sound movement through solids and liquids	2
	the speed of sound and the speed of light	2
describe	uses of ultrasound	any number
design an experiment	to show what types of matter sound travels through, including liquids, solids, and gases	3
diagram	an echo	any number
discuss	the statement "Sound cannot travel in a vacuum."	1
explain	sound as a disturbance in the air, or some other "elastic medium" caused by vibration or shock	1
	the statement "Sound can be heard better and farther on damp, foggy, or cold days."	1
graph	the number of sounds heard in a single minute by criteria established	any number
	decibels of common sounds	any number
illustrate	a sound wave (one compression + one rarefaction)	2
	the human ear as a sound receiver	any number
list	musical instruments, including stringed, wind, and percussion	3
make a table	for the decibels of common sounds (for example, whispering at 10–20 decibels and loud talking at 60 decibels)	any number
question	create a "know?-like to know?-learned?" about sound	3
research	how sound moves by traveling in waves that move in all directions	1
	ways in which sounds differ in pitch, intensity, and quality	3
	sonic booms	4
	the "who, what, when, where" of Christian Johann Doppler, Marin Mersenn, Ernst Mach, Ernst Chladni, Charles E. Yeager	4
show cause and effect	of sound and animal survival	any number

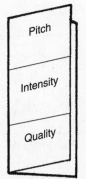

Three-tab book

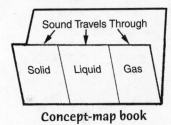

Concept-map book

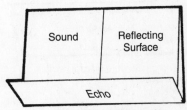

Two-tab matchbook

Half book

Thermal Energy: Heat

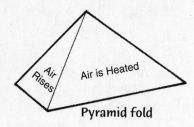
Pyramid fold

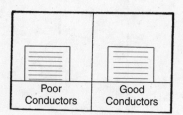
Pocket book

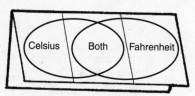
Three-tab Venn diagram

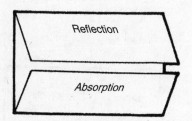
Shutter-fold book

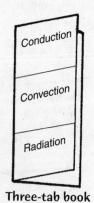
Three-tab book

Skill	Activity Suggestion	Foldable Parts
compare and contrast	light energy and heat energy from the Sun	2
	Celsius and Fahrenheit temperature scales	2
	conduction, convection, and radiation	3
	materials used as conductors and those used as insulators	any number
	surfaces that reflect and absorb heat energy	2
describe	heat radiation as infrared radiation	1
design	an energy-efficient house that will have little heat loss through conduction or convection	any number
design an experiment	to show reflection and absorption of heat radiation on dark and light surfaces	2
diagram	a convection current in a liquid and a convection current in a gas, including that 1) liquids and gases are fluids and they flow, 2) when part of a fluid is warmer than the fluid surrounding it, it rises, 3) the surrounding cooler fluid moves in, and 4) when fluid is warmed, it will rise, etc.	any number
explain	boiling and freezing	2
	how heat is transferred through solids by conduction	1
	the statement "The hotter an object is, the more heat energy it radiates."	1
illustrate	heat transfer, which is energy moving from places with high temperatures to places with lower temperatures	2
list	materials that are either good conductors or poor conductors of heat	2
measure	heat energy	any number
question	create a "know?-like to know?-learned?" about heat	3
research	the three laws of thermodynamics	3
	air as a good insulator and poor conductor (for example, birds fluff their feathers, air between walls, air insulation, and more)	2
	the "what, where, when, how" of determining absolute zero	4
	the "who, what, when, where" of any of the following people: Daniel Gabriel Fahrenheit, Anders Celsius, Benjamin Thompson, James Prescott Joule, William Thomson, Josiah Willard Gibbs	4

Waves

Skill	Activity Suggestion	Foldable Parts
chart	examples of constructive and destructive interference	2
compare and contrast	movement of water waves and light waves	2
	transverse waves and longitudinal waves	2
	compressions and rarefactions	2
define	frequency as the number of waves each second	1
	reflection, refraction, diffraction	3
describe	wavelength, frequency, wave speed, amplitude, and energy	5
diagram	the amplitude and wavelength of a wave	2
explain	how waves transfer energy from one place to another without a substance being transferred or moved	1
make a concept map	of mechanical waves, including transverse and compressional	3
question	create a "know?-like to know?-learned?" about waves	3
research	the "who, what, when, where" of Christian Johann Doppler, Otto von Gueriche, John William Strutt, Louis de Broglie	4
show cause and effect	of high and low wave frequency	2

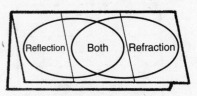

Three-tab Venn diagram

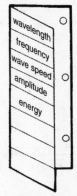

Vocabulary book

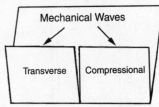

Concept-map book

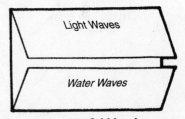

Shutter-fold book

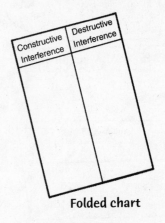

Folded chart

Work and Machines

	Simple Tools
	Lever
	Pulley
	Screw
	Inclined Plane
	Wedge
	Wheel-and-Axle
	History of Simple Tools

Layered book
(4 sheets of paper)

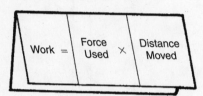

Work = Force Used × Distance Moved

Three-tab book (horizontal)

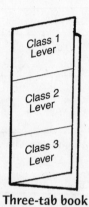

Class 1 Lever

Class 2 Lever

Class 3 Lever

Three-tab book (vertical)

Fixed Pulley | Both | Moveable Pulley

Three-tab Venn diagram

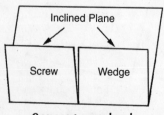

Inclined Plane

Screw | Wedge

Concept-map book

Skill	Activity Suggestion	Foldable Parts
compare and contrast	a fixed pulley and a movable pulley	2
	the work needed to move something up a long, gradual inclined place compared to a short, steep inclined plane	2
	a screw and a spiral staircase	2
	simple machines and compound machines	2
define	work as a force used times distance moved	1
describe	things that can produce forces, including wind, steam, muscles, electricity, gasoline, moving water, sunlight, and more	any number
	a wheel and axle as a lever and show examples	any number
	the function of a wedge	1
diagram	a lever as a rigid bar resting on a fixed point, or fulcrum	any number
explain	the statement "If you push a rock and it doesn't move, work has not been done."	1
identify	simple tools, including lever, pulley, screw, inclined plane, wedge, and wheel-and-axle	6
	three classes of levers, including the following: 1st class—fulcrum between effort force and resistance force; 2nd class—resistance force in middle, effort and resistance force at ends; 3rd class—effort force between the resistance force and fulcrum	3
illustrate	the thread and pitch of a screw	any number
investigate	how machines transfer a force from one place to another, including how some increase the strength of a force, some change the direction of a force, and some increase the distance over which a force acts	3
	effort and resistance as they relate to tools	2
list	compound machines	2
make a timeline	of inventions and technology	any number
question	create a "know?-like to know?-learned?" about work and machines	3
research	the "what, when, where, why" of principles of simple machines	4
	the "who, what, when, where" of Archimedes, Leonardo Da Vinci, James Watt	4
show cause and effect	of friction as it relates to machines	2
write	about situations in which levers perform work	any number

Foldables for Astronomy

The following science topics are covered in this section:

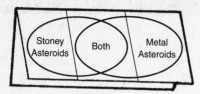

Three-tab Venn diagram

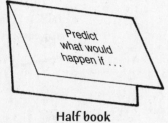

Half book

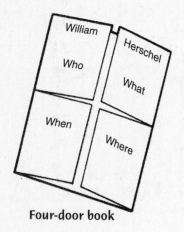

Four-door book

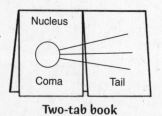

Two-tab book

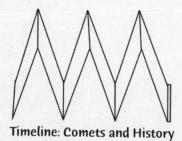

Timeline: Comets and History

Asteroids

Skill	Activity Suggestion	Foldable Parts
compare and contrast	the main types of asteroids, including stony and metal	2
describe	asteroids inside and outside the asteroid belt	2
diagram	the position of the asteroid belt in the solar system	any number
discuss	the most widely accepted theory about the asteroid belt's formation	any number
explain	why asteroids are also called "minor planets," or "planetoids"	1
	how astronomers name asteroids	1
graph	asteroid diameters (Ceres, 623 miles; Pallas, 378 miles; Juno, 143 miles; Astraea, 73 miles; Phocaea, 45 miles)	any number
investigate	the danger inherent in an asteroid crossing Earth's orbit	1
predict	what would happen if a large asteroid hit Earth	any number
question	create a "know?-like to know?-learned?" about asteroids	3
research	the discovery and naming of the first asteroid	1
	for information on the Celestial Police	1
	what we know about past asteroid collisions with Earth, possibly including Chicxulub on the Yucatan Peninsula	any number
	the "what, where, when, how/why" of Kirkwood Gaps and Daniel Kirkwood	4
	the "who, what, when, where" of Giuseppe Piazzi or William Herschel	4

Comets

Skill	Activity Suggestion	Foldable Parts
chart	short-period and long-period comets	2
compare and contrast	a short-period comet and a long period comet	2
diagram	parts of a comet, including nucleus, coma, and tail(s)	3
explain	why a comet's tail always points away from the Sun (because of solar winds)	1
graph	short-period and long-period comets	any number
make a model	of a comet	1
make a table	covering basic information on several known comets, possibly including name, discoverer, first sighting, estimated orbit time, next sighting	any number
make a timeline	of comets viewed throughout history	any number
research	the composition of a comet	any number
	modern and historic comets	any number
	future comet encounters	any number
	the "who, what, where, when" of any of the following people: Edmond Halley, Jean Louis Pons, Fred Lawrence Whipple, Carolyn Shoemaker	4

Earth's Moon

Skill	Activity Suggestion	Foldable Parts
chart	information obtained from missions to the Moon	any number
compare and contrast	planets and satellites	2
	a waxing moon and a waning moon	2
	impact craters on the Moon and Earth	2
	the near side and far side of Earth's Moon	2
	synodic month and sidereal month	2
	lunar eclipse and solar eclipse	2
define	perigee and apogee	2
diagram	geologic features of Earth's Moon, including maria, highlands, craters, mountains, and rilles	any number
	a map of the near side of the Moon, label its major features, and mark sites of lunar landings	any number
discuss	the statement "The Moon is 'dead' but not static. It is still changing."	1
explain	sources of radiated light and reflected light in space	2
	rotation and revolution as it relates to Earth's view of the Moon	2
	how John William Draper was able to take the first photograph of the Moon in 1840	1
graph	heights and depths of different geologic moon features	any number
illustrate	the phases of Earth's Moon	any number
make a timeline	of the discoveries and exploration of Earth's Moon	any number
make a Venn diagram	labeled *Earth's satellite, artificial satellite,* and *both*	3
question	create a "know?-like to know?-learned?" about Earth's Moon	3
research	moon rock composition, including basalt and breccia	2
	theories of the Moon's formation, including simultaneous creation, capture, collision, and fission	4
	the Sea of Tranquility, which is the *Apollo 11* landing sight	1
	legends and folk tales about the Moon	any number
	the "who, what, when, where" of Johannes Hevelius or Eugene Shoemaker	4
show cause and effect	of litter left on the Moon by American and Russian space ventures	2
	of craters on the Moon that have not weathered since impact	2

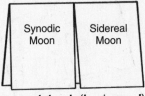

Two-tab book (horizontal)

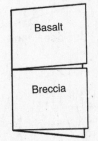

Two-tab book (vertical)

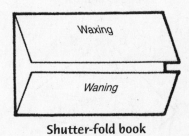

Shutter-fold book

Billboard book

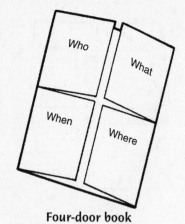

Four-door book

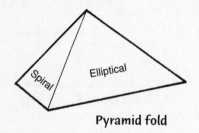

Timeline: History of Space Exploration

Pyramid fold

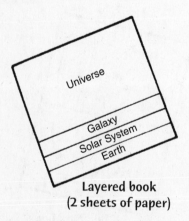

Layered book (2 sheets of paper)

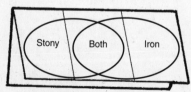

Three-tab Venn diagram

Exploring Space

Skill	Activity Suggestion	Foldable Parts
compare and contrast	crewed and uncrewed space vehicles	2
	the launch of a spacecraft and a space shuttle	2
describe	where space "begins" after leaving Earth's atmosphere	1
diagram	a space probe	any number
explain	how a spacecraft overcomes gravity	1
make a timeline	of space exploration	any number
question	create a "know?-like to know?-learned?" about space exploration	3
research	the problems of life and work in space and present solutions	any number
	the "who, what, when, where" of any of the following people: Robert H. Goddard, Alan B. Shepard, Jr., Yuri A. Gagarin, John Hershal Glenn	4
sequence	the launch events of a spacecraft	any number
	the events of a space shuttle leaving Earth, orbiting Earth, and returning to Earth	3

Galaxies

Skill	Activity Suggestion	Foldable Parts
compare and contrast	barred spiral galaxies and unbarred spirals	2
	galactic clusters and globular clusters	2
describe	spiral galaxies as rotating pinwheels of stars	any number
	Earth and the solar system within the Milky Way	any number
	four discoveries of the Hubble Space Telescope	4
diagram	the Milky Way galaxy side view and from above	2
explain	elliptical galaxies	1
	the use of light-years as a unit of measurement in space	any number
question	create a "know?-like to know?-learned?" about galaxies	3
research	the "who, what, when, where" Harlow Shapley	4
	the Local Group	any number

Meteors and Meteorites

Skill	Activity Suggestion	Foldable Parts
compare and contrast	meteor and meteorite	2
describe	shooting stars as meteors in Earth's atmosphere	any number
	meteroid, meteror, and meteorite	3
diagram	a meteor entering Earth's atmosphere	1
	the sizes of largest known meteorites	any number
	famous meteorite craters worldwide on a map	any number
Make a Venn diagram	types of meteorites	3
predict	what would happen if a large meteorite impacted the ocean	any number
question	create a "know?-like to know?-learned?" about meteors	3
research	the "who, what, when, where" of Daniel Barringer	4
	the Ahnighito Meteorite, or the Shoemaker-Levy 9 comet	1
	myths or legends about meteors and meteorites	any number

Solar System: General

Skill	Activity Suggestion	Foldable Parts
compare and contrast	stars, planets, and satellites	3
	the inner planets and the outer planets	2
	solid planets and gaseous planets	2
	revolution and rotation	2
	selected planets' rotation and revolution	2
	our solar system to another solar system	2
debate	past and present views of the location of Earth in the universe, both geocentric and heliocentric	2
	the question "Could life exist in another solar system?"	2
diagram	the solar system	any number
explain	how planets are affected by distance from the Sun, including atmosphere and revolution period	any number
graph	data about the nine planets	any number
	planets visible to the unaided eye and planets seen only through magnification	any number
make a model	of the inner planets	4
	of the outer planets	5
make a table	of data about the nine known planets	any number
	listing planets, number of satellites, dates they were discovered, and more	any number
make a timeline	of planet discoveries	any number
	of spacecraft development and missions	any number
question	create a "know?-like to know?-learned?" about the solar system	3
research	the Sun and the nine known planets	any number
	mythology as it relates to astronomy, including Apollo, the sun god, Diana, goddess of the Moon, planets named after mythological gods and goddesses	any number
	planets with and without satellites	2
	the most common element in the solar system	1
	the first United States astronauts	any number
	new solar system discoveries	any number
	the "what, where, when, why/how" of any of the historic observatories and instruments dedicated to the study of astronomy, including Arecibo Observatory in Puerto Rico, National Radio Astronomy Observatory in New Mexico, or Keck Observatory in Hawaii	4
	the "who, what, when, where" of any of the following people: Hipparchus, Nicolaus Copernicus, Johannes Kepler, Johann Elert Bode, Pierre Simon de Laplace	4

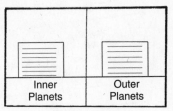

Pocket book

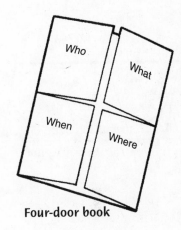

Four-door book

Pyramid mobile:
The Sun and Planets

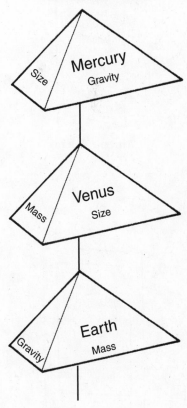

Solar System: Mercury

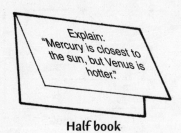

Half book

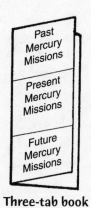

Three-tab Venn diagram

Mercury | Both | Earth

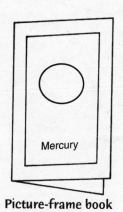

Past Mercury Missions

Present Mercury Missions

Future Mercury Missions

Three-tab book

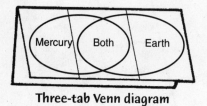

Mercury

Picture-frame book

Skill	Activity Suggestion	Foldable Parts
compare and contrast	Mercury and Earth	2
	Mercury's elliptical orbit in comparison to that of other planets	2
	cross sections of Mercury and Earth	2
debate	sending missions to Mercury	2
diagram	the surface of Mercury	any number
explain	how to identify Mercury, including how it is visible at sunrise and sunset and rides low in the sky	1
	the statement "Mercury is closest to the Sun, but Venus is hotter."	1
graph	the percentage of Mercury's surface that is mapped using a circle graph	any number
	the temperatures of Mercury's surface at the poles and equator	2
	the percentages of Mercury's core versus its crust	any number
hypothesize	the cause of Caloris Basin, a Texas-size crater ringed by mountains	any number
illustrate	Mercury as part of the solar system	any number
question	create a "know?-like to know?-learned?" about Mercury	3
research	how Mercury got its name	1
	past, present, and future Mercury missions	3
	the "what, where, when, why/how" of *Mariner 10*	4

Solar System: Venus

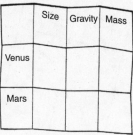

Folded table

Skill	Activity Suggestion	Foldable Parts
compare and contrast	Venus's length of day and year to Earth's	2
	Venus's orbit to the orbits of other planets	any number
	Earth and Venus	2
define	retrograde	1
diagram	the surface of Venus as revealed by the *Magellan* spacecraft	any number
explain	how to identify Venus, including how it shines bright in the sky and is noted for evening and morning appearances	any number
	why the Sun rises in the west and sets in the east on Venus	1
	the statement "Venus is the hottest planet in the solar system."	1
hypothesize	as to the cause of an area called Crater Farm	1
illustrate	Venus as part of the solar system	any number
make a table	for the size, gravity, and mass of Venus and another planet	3
	of data pertaining to missions to Venus	any number
make a timeline	of Venus observations from Earth and space	any number
question	create a "know?-like to know?-learned?" about Venus	3
research	how Venus got its name	1
	why Venus is also called the "evening and morning star"	1
	the clouds covering Venus, including their composition, lightning, and visibility	any number
	the statement "Venus appears to have phases like the Moon."	1
	the "who, what, when, where" of Galilei Galileo or Jeremiah Horrocks	4

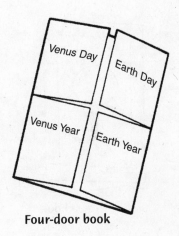

Four-door book

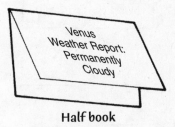

Half book

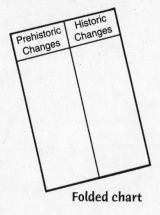

Folded chart

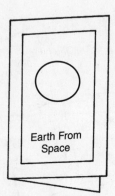

Earth From Space

Picture-frame book

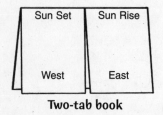

Sun Set	Sun Rise
West	East

Two-tab book

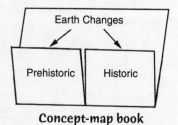

Earth Changes

Prehistoric   Historic

Concept-map book

Earth is "just right"

half book

Solar System: Earth

Skill	Activity Suggestion	Foldable Parts
compare and contrast	Earth's atmospheric composition and that of other planets	2
	an Earth day to a day on another planet	2
	geologic features of Earth and those of another planet	2
describe	Earth as seen from space	1
	how the first photos of Earth from space changed humankind's view of the planet	any number
	the theory of plate tectonics and how it affects Earth's surface	1
explain	why the Sun rises in the east and sets in the west on Earth	1
	Earth is said to be "just right" (not too hot and not too cold)	1
graph	the percentage of land and water on Earth's surface	2
identify	things that make Earth unique from other planets	any number
illustrate	Earth as part of the solar system	any number
	Earth's orbit and compare it to the orbits of other planets	any number
make a table	including the size, gravity, and mass of Earth and Venus	3
make a timeline	of human exploration of planet Earth	any number
prove	the importance of liquid water to life on Earth	any number
question	create a "know?-like to know?-learned?" about Earth	3
research	how Earth got its name	1
	the "who, what, where, when" of any of the following people: Eratosthenes of Cyrene, Claudius Ptolemy, or Seth Carlo Chandler	4

Solar System: Mars

Skill	Activity Suggestion	Foldable Parts
compare and contrast	ancient and current views of Mars	2
	a day and a year on Mars and Earth	2
diagram	the surface of Mars	any number
discuss	the statement "Mars is more hospitable for life than Venus."	1
explain	why humankind expected to find life on Mars	1
	why it would be impossible for humans to breathe on Mars	1
illustrate	Mars as part of the solar system	any number
list	ways in which Mars and Earth are similar and different	any number
make a table	including size, gravity, and mass of Mars and Earth	3
	with data pertaining to missions to Mars	any number
make a timeline	of Mars observations and discoveries	any number
make a Venn diagram	labeled *Phobos, Deimos,* and *both*	3
question	create a "know?-like to know?-learned?" about Mars	3
research	how Mars got its name and why it is called "the red planet"	2
	the composition of the Martian atmosphere	1
	Syrtis Major and Chryse Planitia	2
	the "who, what, when, where" of any of the following people: Asaph Hall, Giovanni Viginio Schiaparelli, or Percival Lowell	4

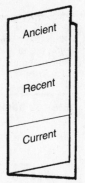

Three-tab flowchart

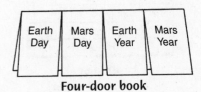

Four-door book

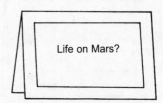

Picture-frame book

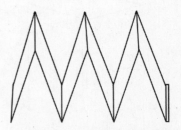

Timeline: History of Mars Exploration

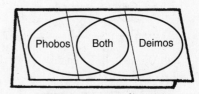

Three-tab Venn diagram

Solar System: Jupiter

Skill	Activity Suggestion	Foldable Parts
compare and contrast	the movement of the Great Red Spot in Jupiter's southern hemisphere and the cyclonic movement in Earth's southern hemisphere	2
	Jupiter's length of day and year to Earth and to another gaseous planet	3
	Jupiter's orbit to that of other planets	any number
debate	sending a crewed mission to Jupiter	2
diagram	the gaseous layers of Jupiter and compare them to another gaseous planet	any number
explain	why Jupiter is said to have weather and describe what it is like	1
hypothesize	as to why Jupiter is both the largest gaseous planet and the first gaseous planet	2
illustrate	Jupiter as part of the solar system	any number
list	similarities between Jupiter and other gaseous planets	any number
make a table	including size, gravity, and mass of Jupiter and Earth	3
	of data pertaining to missions to observe Jupiter	any number
make a timeline	of observations and exploration of Jupiter	any number
question	create a "know?-like to know?-learned?" about Jupiter	3
research	the Great Red Spot	any number
	Jupiter's atmospheric composition	1
	the ring that surrounds Jupiter and compare it to another ringed planet	any number
	the "who, what, when, where" of Galileo Galilei or Robert Hooke	4

Three-tab book

What do you Know about Jupiter? / What would you like to know about Jupiter? / What have you learned about Jupiter?

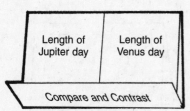

Layered book (4 sheets of paper)

Jupiter Facts / Distance from Sun / Diameter / Moons / Rings / Length of day / Length of year / History

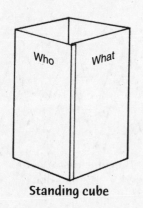

Two-tab matchbook

Length of Jupiter day / Length of Venus day / Compare and Contrast

Who / What

Standing cube

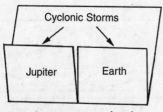

Concept-map book

Cyclonic Storms / Jupiter / Earth

Solar System: Saturn

Skill	Activity Suggestion	Foldable Parts
compare and contrast	Saturn's Great White Spot to Jupiter's Great Red Spot	2
	Saturn's length of day and year to Jupiter's	2
	Saturn's orbit to that of other planets	any number
describe	Cassini's Division	1
diagram	Saturn's rings	any number
explain	why Saturn and Jupiter produce more heat than they receive from the Sun	1
illustrate	Saturn as part of the solar system	any number
list	similarities between Saturn's rings and rings of other planets	any number
make a table	including size, gravity, and mass of Saturn and Earth	3
	of data pertaining to Saturn observations and discoveries	any number
make a timeline	of observations and exploration of Saturn	any number
question	create a "know?-like to know?-learned?" about Saturn	3
research	the Great White Spot	1
	the most recent data on the composition of Saturn's rings	any number
	at least four of Saturn's moons, possibly including Phoebe, Iapetus, Mimas, Enceladus, Janus, Titan	any number
	the "who, what, when, where" of any of the following people: Giovanni Domenico Cassini, Christiaan Huygens, or Johann Franz Encke	4

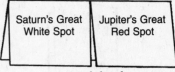

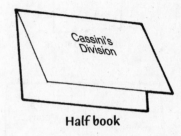

Saturn's Great White Spot   Jupiter's Great Red Spot

Two-tab book

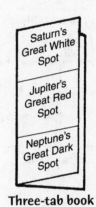

Cassini's Division

Half book

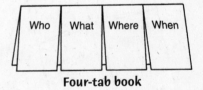

Saturn's Great White Spot

Jupiter's Great Red Spot

Neptune's Great Dark Spot

Three-tab book

Who   What   Where   When

Four-tab book

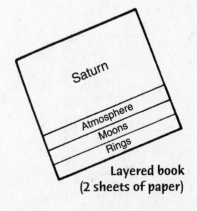

Saturn

Atmosphere

Moons

Rings

Layered book (2 sheets of paper)

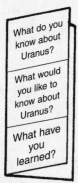

What do you know about Uranus?

What would you like to know about Uranus?

What have you learned?

Three-tab book

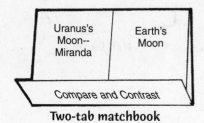

| Uranus's Moon-- Miranda | Earth's Moon |

Compare and Contrast

Two-tab matchbook

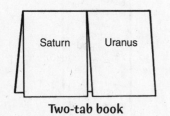

| Saturn | Uranus |

Two-tab book

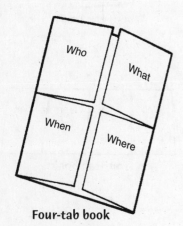

Who | What

When | Where

Four-tab book

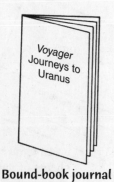

Voyager Journeys to Uranus

Bound-book journal

Solar System: Uranus

Skill	Activity Suggestion	Foldable Parts
compare and contrast	Uranus's length of day and year to Saturn's	2
	Uranus's orbit to that of other planets	any number
	Uranus and other gaseous planets	any number
	the rings that surround Uranus and those that surround Saturn	2
	Uranus's moon Miranda to Earth's Moon	2
diagram	the gaseous layers of Uranus and compare them to other gaseous planets	any number
explain	how the discovery of Uranus doubled the known solar system's size	1
make a table	showing size, gravity, and mass of Uranus and Earth	3
	of information about Uranus's moon	any number
make a timeline	of observations and discoveries of Uranus	any number
question	create a "know?-like to know?-learned?" about Uranus	3
research	the discovery of Uranus	1
	Uranus's atmospheric composition	1
	new information learned from the *Voyager* journeys	any number
	the "who, what, where, when" of William Herschel	4

Solar System: Neptune

Skill	Activity Suggestion	Foldable Parts
chart	information concerning Neptune's moons	any number
compare and contrast	Neptune's length of day and year to Uranus's	2
	Neptune's orbit to that of other planets	any number
	Neptune and other gaseous planets	any number
	Neptune's moon Triton to Earth's Moon	2
diagram	the five barely visible rings that surround Neptune and compare them to Saturn's rings	any number
explain	why Neptune looks blue	1
illustrate	Neptune as part of the solar system	any number
make a table	including size, gravity, and mass of Neptune and Earth	3
	of Neptune observations and discoveries	any number
make a timeline	of observations and exploration of Neptune	any number
question	create a "know?-like to know?-learned?" about Neptune	3
research	the Great Dark Spot	1
	Neptune's atmospheric composition	any number
	the "who, what, when, where" of any of the following people: Urbain Jean Leverrier, Johann G. Galle, or John Couch Adams	4

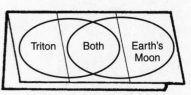

Three-tab Venn diagram

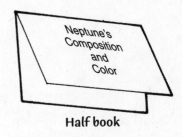

Half book

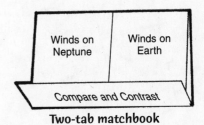

Folded table

Two-tab matchbook

Know about Pluto

Like to know about Pluto

Learned about Pluto

Three-tab book

Pluto's Moon: Charon

Picture-frame book

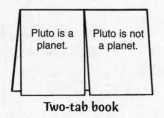

Pluto is a planet.

Pluto is not a planet.

Two-tab book

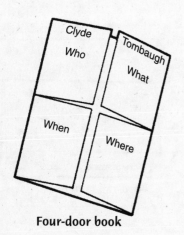

Clyde Who

Tombaugh What

When

Where

Four-door book

Solar System: Pluto

Skill	Activity Suggestion	Foldable Parts
compare and contrast	Pluto's composition to rocky and gaseous planets	any number
	size, gravity, and mass of Pluto and Earth	3
	Pluto's length of day and year to Neptune's	2
	Pluto's orbit to that of other planets	any number
	Pluto and other planets	any number
debate	whether Pluto is a planet	2
explain	how Pluto got its name	1
make a table	of data pertaining to missions to Pluto	any number
make a timeline	of observations and discoveries of Pluto	any number
question	create a "know?-like to know?-learned?" about Pluto	3
research	Pluto's atmospheric conditions	any number
	Pluto's moon, Charon	1
	the controversy over Pluto's classification	1
	the "who, what, where, when" of Percival Lowell or Clyde Tombaugh	4

Stars

Skill	Activity Suggestion	Foldable Parts
chart	apparent magnitudes	any number
	absolute magnitudes (how stars are compared as to how bright they would look if they were an equal distance from Earth)	any number
compare and contrast	star colors and temperatures, including blue, white, yellow, orange, and red stars	2
	novas and supernovas	2
	apparent magnitude and absolute magnitude	2
	constellations and asterisms	2
diagram	sizes of stars, including supergiants, red giants, blue main-sequence stars, medium-sized stars, white dwarfs, neutron stars, yellow dwarf, red dwarf, and black dwarf	8
	the cross-section of a typical star	any number
	binary stars and star clusters	2
explain	the significance of star spectra, including O, B, A, F, G, K, and M	any number
	two ways stars are documented, including numbered catalog identifications and names	2
	why there are only 88 constellations	1
graph	percentages of the most common chemical elements in stars, including hydrogen, helium, and other trace elements	3
list	examples of absolute magnitudes from brightest to least bright stars, possibly including Rigel at −7.1, Betelgeuse at −5.6, Sirius at +1.4, and the Sun at +4.8	any number
outline	the life of a star	any number
question	create a "know?-like to know?-learned?" about stars	3
research	how stars produce energy	1
	four of the brightest stars observed, possibly including Sirius, Canopus, Arcturus, Rigel, Vega, Pollux, Procyon, Regulus, and Stella	4
	Sirius, the brightest star in our night sky, and its importance to ancient Egypt	1
	the North Star's use for navigation in the northern hemisphere in the past and present	2
	the "who, what, where, when" of any of the following people: Jipparchus, Johann Bayer, Edward Emerson Barnard, Annie Jump Cannon, Henrietta Leavitt, Cecilia Payne-Gaposchkin, Hans Albrecht Bethe, Margaret Burbidge	4
sequence	six stars from the closest to most distant, possibly including the Sun, Proxima Centauri, Alpha Centauri, Bernard's star, Wolf 359, Lalande 21185, Luyten 726-8A and 726-8B, Sirius A, Sirius B, and Ross 154	6

Three-tab book (vertical)

Two-tab book

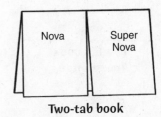

Three-tab Venn diagram

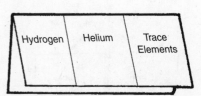

Three-tab book (horizontal)

Layered book (4 sheets of paper)

Sun

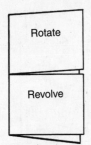

Two-tab book (vertical)

Rotate

Revolve

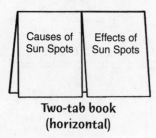

Two-tab book (horizontal)

Causes of Sun Spots

Effects of Sun Spots

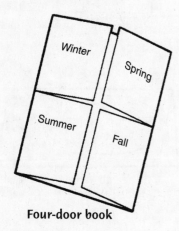

Four-door book

Winter

Spring

Summer

Fall

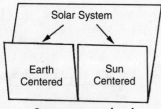

Concept-map book

Solar System

Earth Centered

Sun Centered

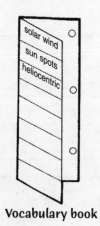

Vocabulary book

solar wind

sun spots

heliocentric

Skill	Activity Suggestion	Foldable Parts
chart	purposes of the ozone layer	any number
compare and contrast	the Sun to other stars	2
	rotation and revolution	2
	theories of a Sun-centered solar system and an Earth-centered solar system through history	2
	the sizes of the Sun and Earth	2
	the use of solar energy to energy produced by fossil fuels	2
	solar energy use in the past and present	2
describe	why the Sun appears to rise and set	2
	the importance of the Sun as a source of energy, including how it gives Earth sunlight, moonlight, photosynthesis, weather patterns, the water cycle, and wind	any number
diagram	a cross-section of the Sun	any number
explain	the Sun's role in Earth's seasonal changes	1
	moonlight as reflected sunlight	1
	how leaves are food factories powered by the Sun	1
graph	the percentages of hydrogen and helium that compose the Sun	2
	the percentage of the Sun's radiant energy reaching Earth's surface	any number
make a model	comparing our Sun to another star in the Milky Way	2
make a timeline	for Sun discoveries	any number
predict	future uses of solar energy	any number
question	create a "know?-like to know?-learned?" about the Sun	3
research	the time it takes the Sun's light to reach Earth	1
	measurements of distances in AU	1
	sunspot cycles and their effects	any number
	solar winds	1
	myths and folklore pertaining to the Sun	any number
	the "who, what, where, when" of any of the following people: Hans Bethe, Francis Bailey, Pierre Jules Jansses, or George Ellery Hale	4
show cause and effect	of solar flares	2
	of sunspots	2

Universe

Skill	Activity Suggestion	Foldable Parts
debate	whether the universe is infinite or finite	2
define	the universe	1
describe	views on the size of the universe in the past and present	2
explain	what scientists mean when they speak of "dark matter"	4
make a concept map	including universe, galaxy superclusters, galaxy clusters, galaxies, stars	5
make a timeline	for discoveries relating to our understanding of the universe	any number
question	create a "know?-like to know?-learned?" about the universe	3
research	the most current information on measurements of the most distant, known galaxies	any number
	theories on universe expansion or contraction	2
	how astronomers determine distance to objects in space that are moving away from Earth	1
	quasars and black holes	2
	how long it will take *Voyager 2* to get to the edge of our solar system and try to calculate about how long it would take *Voyager 2* to travel beyond our galaxy	2
	the "what, where, when, why/how" of the Andromeda galaxy	4
	the "who, what, where, when" of any of the following people: Harlow Shapley, Edwin Powell Hubble, geroge Gamow, Bart Jan Bok, or Stephen William Hawking	4
write	about an expanding universe, including how the space between galaxies would be getting farther apart, but not the space between the stars within a galaxy	1

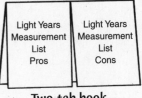

Two-tab book

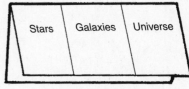

Three-tab book

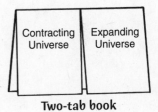

Two-tab book

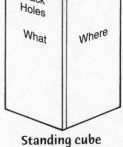

Standing cube

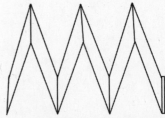

Timeline: Discoveries Relating to Our Understanding of the Universe

Foldables for Earth Science

The following science topics are covered in this section:

Atmosphere

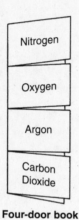

Layered book
(3 sheets of paper)

Skill	Activity Suggestion	Foldable Parts
compare and contrast	the troposphere to another layer	2
	air pressure at sea level and on a mountain top	2
explain	why density of the atmosphere decreases, or air gets thinner, as height increases	1
	ways in which the atmosphere would differ if humans had never lived on Earth	any number
	the statement "The troposphere is the only layer in which life is found naturally."	1
graph	atmosphere composition, including nitrogen (78%), oxygen (21%), argon, and others (1%)	any number
	the troposphere, which contains 75% of the total mass of the atmosphere	any number
hypothesize	as to what the troposphere is and check your assumption	1
identify	the four most common atmospheric gases: nitrogen, oxygen, argon, and carbon dioxide	4
investigate	the similarities and differences between aurora borealis (northern lights) and aurora australis (southern lights)	2
	early attempts to explore and understand Earth's atmosphere	any number
	the layers of the atmosphere, which include troposphere, stratosphere, mesosphere, thermosphere, and exosphere	5
	the troposphere as the "weather" layer	1
question	create a "know?-like to know?-learned?" about Earth's atmosphere	3
research	five common and uncommon particulates found in the atmosphere, including salt, smoke, dust, pollutants, and volcanic ash	5
	the "what, where, when, and why" of objects used in atmospheric research	4
	the "who, what, when, and where" of atmospheric research scientists	4
	the "who, what, when, and where" of James Alfred Van Allen	4
show cause and effect	of industrialization on atmosphere composition	1
	of high and low pressure	2
	of the ozone layer in the stratosphere	2

Nitrogen

Oxygen

Argon

Carbon Dioxide

Four-door book

Air Pressure on a Mountain

Air Pressure at Sea Level

Two-tab book

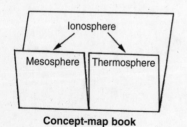

Concept-map book

Caves

Skill	Activity Suggestion	Foldable Parts
compare and contrast	precipitation and dissolution in caves	2
	the inside and outside of a cave, possibly including temperature, life, or light	2
	dry and wet cave systems	2
	past and present use of cave systems by humankind	2
debate	cave systems being opened to tourism	2
describe	common speleothems, including stalactites, stalagmites, and columns	3
determine	carbonic acid's effect on limestone	1
diagram	solution caves, sea caves, and lava caves	3
	the cross-section of an imaginary limestone cave system and label, including sink holes, galleries, caverns, and speleothems	any number
	on a map record the locations of caves around the world, possibly including the longest, deepest, coldest, or largest caverns	any number
explain	how carbonic acid equals carbon dioxide gas plus water	1
graph	lengths of speleothems (stalactities and stalagmites)	2
	cave depth, average temperature, and lengths	3
make a model	of a cave	any number
make a table	of information about famous caves, possibly including average temperature, depths, type of cave, or date of discovery	any number
make a Venn diagram	of cave zones, labeled *light zone, twilight zone,* and *midnight zone*	3
	labeled *dry caves, wet caves,* and *both*	3
prove	the statement "Caves have their own climate."	any number
question	create a "know?-like to know?-learned?" about caves	3
research	one of the world's famous cave systems, possibly Kentucky's Mammoth Cave, Borneo's Sarawak Chamber, or Carlsbad Caverns	any number
	carbonic acid and its part in cave formation	1
	four unique speleothems, possibly including drapery, flowstone, gypsum flowers, or helictites	4
	troglobites, possibly including blind or eyeless beetles, fish, salamanders, or spiders	any number
	endangered cave life	any number
show cause and effect	of groundwater erosion and cave formation	any number

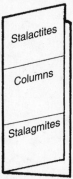

Three-tab book

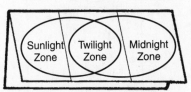

Folded table

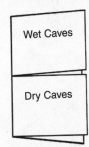

Three-tab Venn diagram

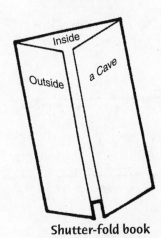

Two-tab book

Shutter-fold book

Dinosaurs

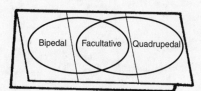

Sir Richard Owen

What
When
Where

**Layered book
(2 sheets of paper)**

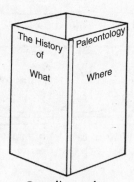

Bipedal | Facultative | Quadrupedal

Three-tab Venn diagram

The History of

Paleontology

What

Where

Standing cube

Triassic

Jurassic

Pyramid fold

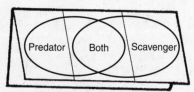

Predator | Both | Scavenger

Three-tab Venn diagram

Skill	Activity Suggestion	Foldable Parts
chart	meat-eaters and plant-eaters	2
compare and contrast	the movement of animals with an upright posture to those with a sprawling posture	2
	several of the giant plant-eating dinosaurs	any number
	Megalosaurus, Giganotosaurus, Carcharodontosaurus, and Tyrannosaurus rex and graph by size	4
	dinosaur movement, including bipedal, quadrapedal, and facultative (movement using both feet)	3
	the sizes of dinosaur eggs to the eggs of living animals	2
	past and present theories on the purpose of Stegosaurus's plates	2
debate	the cost of studying dinosaurs and other prehistoric animals	2
	dinosaur body temperature	2
	the statement "There are some things we will never know conclusively about dinosaurs, such as skin color, sounds, smells, and mannerisms."	2
discuss	how scientists learn from petrified feces with no body fossils to provide clues, including the following: 1) determine when it was deposited, 2) determine dinosaurs that lived at the same time and in the same area, 3) determine if it was deposited by a meat eater or a plant eater	3
	the cause and consequence of being a gigantotherm	2
	an extinction theory	1
explain	the numerical scale of geologic time (for example, dinosaurs lived 248 million years ago to 65 million years ago)	any number
	the importance of fossilized feces	1
	why it is difficult to determine if a dinosaur was omnivorous	1
	why it is difficult to determine if a dinosaur was a predator, a scavenger, or both (for example, Tyrannosaurus rex diet debate)	1
	why most dinosaur fossils are found in areas of terrestrial sedimentation, such as rivers, lakes, or deltas	1
graph	dinosaur sizes from smallest to largest known	any number
	length of dinosaur body parts, possibly including necks, tails, claws, heads, or plates	any number
illustrate	animals that are often incorrectly called dinosaurs, possibly including Dimetrodon, pterosaurs, and swimming reptiles	any number
	outlines of different-shaped dinosaur teeth, including peg, leaflike, large and small, sharp and/or serrated, and batteries of teeth	any number
list	advantages and disadvantages of being cold blooded and warm blooded	2
	three characteristics of amniotic eggs, including hard-shelled, embryo surrounded by a liquid, and an amnion membrane	3
	the advantages and disadvantages of different dinosaur defense techniques, including armor, scutes, horns, whiplike tails, and giant size	any number

Dinosaurs, *continued*

Skill	Activity Suggestion	Foldable Parts
make a chart	to classify and record dinosaurs studied, including phylum, class, order, family, genus, and species (for example: Chordata, Reptilia, Theropoda, Tyrannosauridae, Tyrannosaurus rex)	6
make a timeline	of the Mesozoic Era	any number
make a Venn diagram	labeled *carnivorous, herbivorous,* and *omnivorous*	3
	labeled *predators, scavengers,* and *possibly both*	3
	labeled *bipedal, quadrapedal,* and *facultative*	3
outline	the commercialization of dinosaurs since they were first named in 1842	any number
question	create a "know?-like to know?-learned?" about dinosaurs	3
research	the two divisions that contain nearly all known dinosaurs (Saurischia and Ornithischia)	2
	dinosaurs that are neither Saurischia nor Ornithischia	2
	the past and present views of dinosaur stances, including tail position and posture	2
	the importance of ichnites and track ways	2
	flora of the Mesozoic Era, including Triassic, Jurassic, and Cretaceous	3
	dinosaur discoveries on each of the seven continents	7
	five examples of dinosaur trace fossils, including eggs, nests, footprints, skin imprints, and feces	5
	mummified dinosaurs	any number
	famous fossilized nesting sites, called rookeries	any number
	the "who, what, where, when" of any of the following people: Gideon and Mary Ann Mantall, Sir Richard Owen, Othniel Charles Marsh, Edward Drinker Cope	4

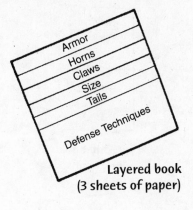

Layered book
(3 sheets of paper)

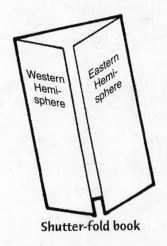

Shutter-fold book

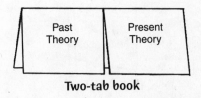

Two-tab book

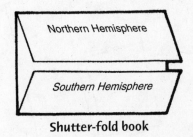

Shutter-fold book

Earth

Two-tab book (vertical)

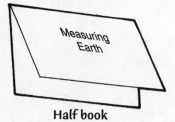

Half book

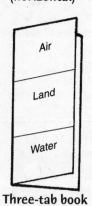

Two-tab book (horizontal)

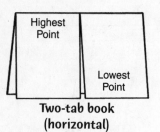

Three-tab book

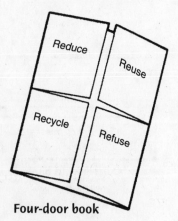

Four-door book

Skill	Activity Suggestion	Foldable Parts
chart	renewable, nonrenewable, and inexhaustible energy resources	3
compare and contrast	hydrosphere, lithosphere, and atmosphere	3
	renewable and nonrenewable energy resources	2
	Earth's cultural development and technological development	2
debate	alternative energy sources, including water, wind, solar, nuclear, and geothermal	5
describe	Earth as part of the universe, the Milky Way galaxy, and the solar system	3
	Earth in terms of water and land	2
diagram	Earth's shape as it relates to polar and equatorial circumference	2
	Earth's interior	any number
discuss	the four Rs of ecology: reduce, reuse, recycle, refuse	4
explain	sidereal day and sidereal year	2
graph	Earth's surface area (70.8% water and 29.2% land)	2
make a model	of planet Earth as part of the solar system	any number
make a timeline	of Earth's geological development and change	any number
question	create a "know?-like to know?-learned?" about planet Earth	3
research	Earth's movement, including rotation, revolution around the Sun, traveling through the galaxy in the solar system	any number
	ancient myths and folklore about Earth's formation	any number
	how Earth's size is measured	1
	how scientists determine the age of Earth	1
	the difference between Earth's diameter at its poles and the equator	2
	Earth's three main fossil fuels (oil, gas, and coal)	3
	the percentages of pollution in the air, land, and water	3
	the "who, what, where, when" of Beno Guttenberg	4
show cause and effect	of air, land, and water pollution	3

Earthquakes

Skill	Activity Suggestion	Foldable Parts
compare and contrast	the Richter Scale and Mercalli Scale	2
	recent and historic earthquakes in a specific region	2
	the earthquake belt that circles the Pacific Ocean and the earthquake belt that stretches from the Mediterranean mountains and northern Africa into southern Asia	2
define	tsunami	1
describe	an imaginary town before and after a tsunami	2
diagram	earthquake zones on a map	any number
	major cities in earthquake zones on a map	any number
	the major earthquake bands	any number
	an earthquake	any number
illustrate	a geographic location before and after an earthquake	2
invent	a means of measuring vibrations, such as those produced by a washing machine or a clothes dryer	any number
make a chart	of the Richter Scale	10
	of the Mercalli Scale	12
make a table	listing information about major earthquakes across the world	any number
make a timeline	for the history of detecting and measuring earthquakes	any number
make a Venn diagram	labeled *earthquakes, tsunamis,* and *both*	3
predict	what might happen to your town in the event of a major earthquake	any number
question	create a "know?-like to know?-learned?" about earthquakes	3
research	historic and recent tsunamis	2
	earthquake prediction	any number
	the "what, where, when, why" of the 1995 earthquake in Kobe, Japan	4
	construction techniques for lessening damage and loss of life	any number
	building materials made for earthquake-prone areas	any number
	the "who, what, when, where" of any of the following people: Giuseppe Mercalli, John Milne, Andrija Mohorovicic, Charles Francis Richter	4
show cause and effect	of plate tectonics and earthquakes	2
	of the San Andreas fault	2
write	an earthquake safety manual	1

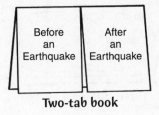

Two-tab book

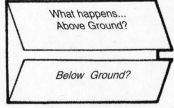

Shutter-fold book

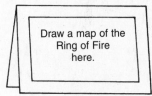

Picture-frame book

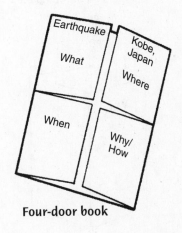

Four-door book

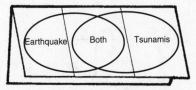

Three-tab Venn diagram

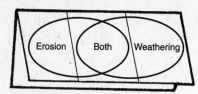

Three-tab Venn diagram

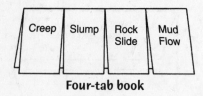

Four-tab book

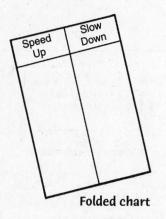

Folded chart

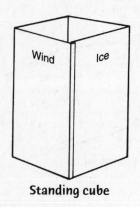

Standing cube

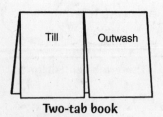

Two-tab book

Erosion and Deposition

Skill	Activity Suggestion	Foldable Parts
compare and contrast	types of ocean sediments, including hydrogenous, biogenous, and lithogenous	3
	fast and slow runoff	2
debate	building groins to protect beaches	2
define	till	2
describe	the beneficial and harmful effects of erosion and deposition	any number
	wave erosion	1
diagram	the formation and movement of a sand dune	2
	how erosion occurs when a continental or valley glacier moves	any number
discuss	how erosion shapes Earth's surface	1
explain	why mass-movement erosion often occurs near volcanoes	1
	erosion as a natural process that humans can speed up or slow down	2
make a concept map	including the four types of mass movements: creep, slump, rock slides, and mudflows	4
make a Venn diagram	labeled *erosion, weathering,* and *both*	3
observe	erosion taking place in your community	any number
question	create a "know?-like to know?-learned?" about erosion and deposition	3
research	current events on mass-movement erosion, called landslides	any number
	information on at least three farming techniques that decrease erosion, possibly including no-till, terracing, conservation tillage, cover crops, contour plowing, or strip cropping	3
	the ways in which glaciers erode rocks	any number
	why caves usually form in sedimentary rock	1
	the economic consequences of beach erosion	any number
	the "what, where, when, why/how" of the Dust Bowl in the 1930s, the Mississippi River delta, or the glacial moraine in Long Island, New York	4
sequence	several different erosion events, including what type of weathering took place, how the weathered material moved to another location, and what happened to it once it was deposited	3
	the formation of rills, gullies, and streams	3
show cause and effect	of agents of erosion, including wind, water, ice, and gravity	4
	of glacial erosion and the number of lakes found in Canada and the northern United States	any number
	of strong winds that carry sediment	2

Fossils

Skill	Activity Suggestion	Foldable Parts
chart	common fossil remains of vertebrates and invertebrates	2
compare and contrast	trace fossils and body fossils	2
	types of fossils by their formation, including mold, cast, petrified, and carbon film	any number
	marine sedimentation and terrestrial sedimentation and plants and animal fossils found in each	any number
	mineralized fossils and cast fossils	2
	mineralized fossils and ancient life forms preserved in ice, permafrost, or bogs	3
	paleontology and archaeology	2
diagram	the axial portion of a skeleton, including the skull, backbone, and tail	3
	a skeleton	any number
discuss	a fossil using the terms anterior, posterior, dorsal, and ventral	4
explain	what type of rock most fossils are found in and why	1
	mineralization and how long it takes	1
illustrate	bones common to all vertebrates	any number
	the formation of a mold fossil	any number
	the formation of a cast fossil	any number
make a Venn diagram	labeled *cast fossil, mold fossil,* and *both*	3
outline	steps for fossilization, including death, decay, burial, and mineralization	4
	sedimentation or sedimentary rock formation, including sediment deposited, compacted, and cementation	3
question	create a "know?-like to know?-learned?" about fossils	3
research	four vertebrate trace fossils, possibly including eggs, tracks, coprolites, skin imprints, or gastroliths	
	common vertebrate body fossils	any number
	different ways in which fossils are dated	any number
	plants and animals preserved in amber	any number
	fossils found in tar pits	any number
	preservation in ice, permafrost, and bogs	3
	the principle of superposition	2
	biostratigraphy	any number
	the "who, what, where, when" of any of the following people: Georg Bauer Agricola, Alexandre Brongniart, Charles Lyell	4

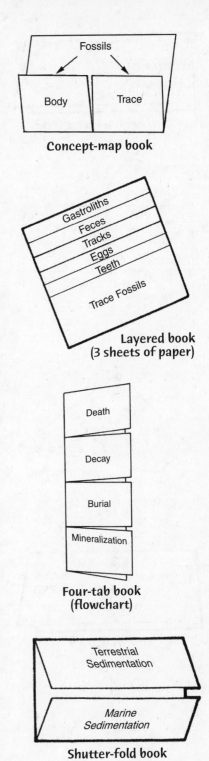

Concept-map book

Layered book (3 sheets of paper)

Four-tab book (flowchart)

Shutter-fold book

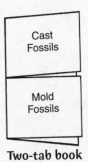

Two-tab book

Geologic Time

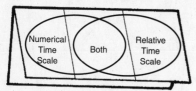

Three-tab Venn diagram

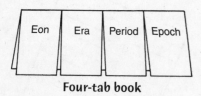

Four-tab book

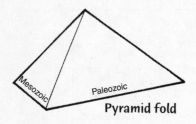

Pyramid fold

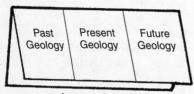

Three-tab book

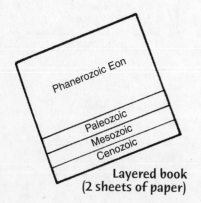

Layered book (2 sheets of paper)

Skill	Activity Suggestion	Foldable Parts
chart	three eons, including Archean, Proterozoic, and Phanerozoic	3
	examples of common organisms from each of the periods of the Mesozoic Era	3
compare and contrast	the shape and size of the world's oceans, past and present	2
	the geologic past and present of the region in which you live and predict its geological future	3
debate	the pros and cons of numerical and relative time scales	2
define	eon, era, period, and epoch	4
describe	the use of boreholes (for example, Project Mohole)	1
diagram	the movement of Earth's plates over the last 400 million years	any number
discuss	problems and solutions of dating rocks and fossils	any number
explain	the purpose of a relative time scale, which states whether something is older or younger than something else	1
	the purpose of a numerical time scale	1
	most geologic time scales combine numerical and relative scales	1
	how radioactive decay of some atoms can be used to date fossils	1
graph	a relative time scale of selected species	any number
list	advantages and disadvantages of one giant continent and one giant ocean	2
	advantages and disadvantages of divided continents to living organisms	2
question	create a "know?-like to know?-learned?" about geologic time	3
research	the eras of the Phanerozoic Eon	3
	current information on Pangaea	any number
	the "who, what, where, when" of Bertram B. Boltwood or Alfred Wegener	4

Glaciers and Ice on Earth

Skill	Activity Suggestion	Foldable Parts
compare and contrast	valley glaciers, ice sheets, and ice shelves	3
	past and present ice coverage	2
	icebergs in the northern and southern oceans	2
debate	the statement "We are living in an intergalacial period"	2
describe	how snow falling in central Antarctica will eventually be at the edge of the continent and possibly part of an iceberg at sea	any number
	the formation of an ice cave	1
design an experiment	to show that ice floats because it is less dense than water	any number
diagram	Greenland, Antarctica, and the Arctic Ocean on a map	3
	the regions of Earth covered in ice during the last Ice Age	any number
explain	the consequences of millions of tons of ice, rocks, and debris moving across a continent	1
	the statement "Long Island is a glacial moraine."	1
	why the majority of the world's lakes are in the northern hemisphere	1
	the effect of meltwater	1
graph	how much of Earth is covered by ice (about 10 percent of land and 12 percent of all ocean)	2
	the division of an iceberg (about 10% above water and 90% below)	2
	the location of freshwater on Earth (90% in Antarctica and Greenland)	any number
illustrate	the formation of a valley glacier	any number
	nunataks, which are mountains sticking through a glacier	any number
	an iceberg above and below water	2
make a timeline	of the life of a glacier, including formation, movement, melting, or calving	3
	of the Ice Ages	any number
predict	what would happen if glacial melting accelerated	any number
	percentages of ice coverage in Earth's future	any number
question	create a "know?-like to know?-learned?" about glaciation	3
research	glacial moraines, glacial lakes, and erratics	3
	kinds of moraines, including terminal, subglacial, englacial, ablation, medial, and lateral	6
	icebergs as a hazard to shipping	any number
	erratic rocks found throughout the northern hemisphere	any number
	the "who, what, when, where" of Jean Louis Agassiz or Albrecht Penck	4
show cause and effect	of ice-covered land and ice-covered ocean	2
	of glacial movement	2
	of glacial movement and lake formation	2
	glacial moraines deposited on land versus those deposited on the seafloor	2

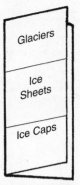

Three-tab book

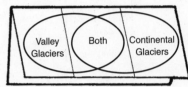

Three-tab Venn diagram

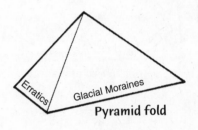

Pyramid fold

Circle graph

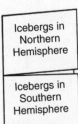

Two-tab book

Land Forms: Mountains, Plains, and Plateaus

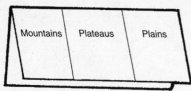

Three-tab book

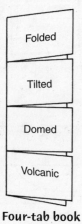

Folded

Tilted

Domed

Volcanic

Four-tab book

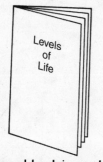

Young   Mature   Old

Three-tab Venn diagram

Levels of Life

Bound-book journal

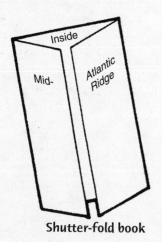

Inside

Mid-   Atlantic Ridge

Shutter-fold book

Skill	Activity Suggestion	Foldable Parts
chart	plants and animals common to a specific mountain ecosystem	any number
	plants and animals common to a plains ecosystem	2
compare and contrast	mountain ranges and mountain chains	2
	the rock layers of mountains and plains	2
	plains and plateaus	2
diagram	the levels of plant and animal life on a mountain	any number
	major plains and plateaus on a world map	any number
explain	the formation and location of folded mountains	any number
	the formation and location of tilted or fault-blocked mountains	any number
	the formation and location of upwarped mountains	any number
graph	the percentage of the world's land that is mountainous	any number
	the percentage of the world's land that is plains or grasslands	2
illustrate	ways in which mountains are formed, including folding, tilting, upwarping, and volcanic activity	4
	the life cycle of a mountain	any number
	mesas and buttes	2
make a Venn diagram	labeled *young mountain*, *mature mountain*, and *old mountain*	3
	for plateaus labeled *young*, *mature*, and *old*	3
question	create a "know?-like to know?-learned?" about landforms	3
research	volcanic mountains	any number
	young mountains	any number
	mature mountains	any number
	old mountains	any number
	the Mid-Atlantic ridge as the world's longest mountain chain	any number
	myths and folktales related to mountains	any number
	mountain-climbing equipment needed and describe safety precautions that must be taken before climbing Mt. Everest	any number
	different kinds of plains, including coastal, interior, and lake	3
	the "who, what, where, when" of any of the following people: James Hall, Clarence Edward Dutton, William Morris Davis	4

Minerals

Skill	Activity Suggestion	Foldable Parts
compare and contrast	surface mining and underground mining	2
debate	the statement "Minerals are the most common solid material on Earth."	2
	surface mining	2
describe	four main characteristics of minerals, including color, luster, cleavage, and hardness	4
design an experiment	to determine if substances have the following four features and therefore are minerals: 1) found in nature, 2) have definite chemical composition wherever found, 3) atoms are arranged in a regular pattern forming solid crystals, 4) usually made up of inorganic substances	4
determine	if all substances in food and water that are called minerals are really minerals (for example, calcium, iron, and phosphorus are called minerals but they are not considered minerals by mineralogists)	1
diagram	where mineral deposits are located on each continent on a map	any number
explain	which minerals are found on Mercury, Venus, Earth, and Mars	4
	the difference between how the word "mineral" is used and its true definition	2
	why coal is not a mineral using the four criteria for minerals	4
	why many gemstones and ores are found in igneous rock	1
hypothesize	why some minerals are prized. Possible answers could include color, purity, brilliance, hardness, scarcity, and demand	any number
investigate	mineral cleavage	any number
list	examples of common and rare minerals	2
	examples of minerals with metallic and nonmetallic luster	2
make a table	illustrating the Mohs scale of mineral hardness	10
question	create a "know?-like to know?-learned?" about minerals	3
research	what rocks, salt, and pencil lead have in common	3
	the importance of ores to humankind in the past and present	2
	what mineral rights are and what minerals they refer to	1
	identification tests for minerals besides color, hardness, cleavage, and luster, possibly including touch, taste, smell, streak test, and chemical tests	any number
	how minerals form	any number
	the "who, what, where, when" of any of the following people: Abraham Gottlob Werner, Friedrich Mohs, William Hallower Miller, Jons Jakob Berzelius	4

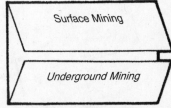

Four-tab book

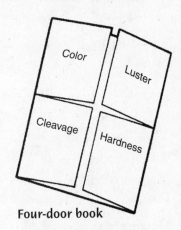

Shutter-fold book

Four-door book

Mohs Scale of Hardness	
1	6
2	7
3	8
4	9
5	10
History of Mineralology	
Vocabulary	

Layered book
(4 sheets of paper with 5 flaps cut in half to make 10 tabs)

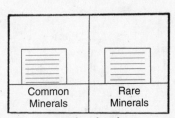

Pocket book

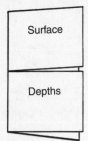

Surface

Depths

Two-tab book (vertical)

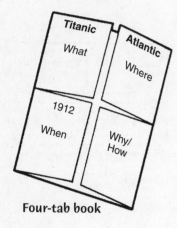

Titanic

What

Atlantic

Where

1912

When

Why/ How

Four-tab book

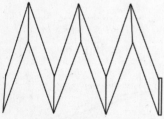

Timeline: History of Oceanography

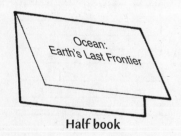

Ocean: Earth's Last Frontier

Half book

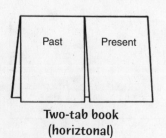

Past

Present

Two-tab book (horiztonal)

Ocean Exploration

Skill	Activity Suggestion	Foldable Parts
debate	the cost of searching for buried treasure and marine salvage	2
discuss	the statement "The ocean is Earth's last frontier."	any number
explain	ways in which the world's oceans would be different today if humans had never existed on Earth	any number
make a model	of an early ocean-going vessel	any number
make a timeline	of oceanography as a science	any number
	of ocean surface exploration	any number
	for the evolution of diving equipment	any number
outline	the history of the exploration of the ocean's depths	any number
question	create a "know?-like to know?-learned?" about ocean exploration	3
research	past and present methods for "viewing" ocean depths, possibly including sonar, radar, cameras, and submersibles	2
	tales of ocean exploration	any number
	life aboard ocean-going vessels in the past and present, possibly including food storage, sleeping arrangements, clothing, and personal space and possessions of sailors	2
	songs sung by early sailors	any number
	the "what, where, when, why/how" of any of the following topics: H.M.S. Challenger, Alvin, Ocean Drilling Program, Titanic	4
	the "who, what, where, when" of any of the following people: Pytheas, Robert D. Ballard, Jacques-Yves Cousteau	4
		4
sequence	events of the ship Titanic	any number
show cause and effect	of exploration by sea in the past and present, possibly including economics, search of new lands, trade routes, and spread of religion	any number
	of countries having powerful navies	2

Ocean Shelf, Slope, and Floor

Skill	Activity Suggestion	Foldable Parts
compare and contrast	continental land to continental margin	2
	types of ocean sediments, including hydrogenous, biogenous, and lithogenous	3
	abyssal plains and abyssal hills	2
debate	ocean floor mining	2
	drilling for oil through ocean crust	2
describe	seamounts and guyots	2
diagram	a cross-section of the ocean, showing land, shelf, slope, and floor	4
	the largest and longest ridges in each ocean on a map	any number
	the continental margin, including shelf, slope, and continental rise	3
	submarine volcanoes	any number
discuss	why the Moon's surface is said to be better known to scientists than the ocean floor	1
explain	the formation of the manganese nodules found on the ocean floor and their commercial importance	2
graph	depths of the deepest trenches in each ocean	any number
make a model	of the ocean floor	any number
question	create a "know?-like to know?-learned?" about the ocean shelf, slope, and floor	3
research	ocean ridges and ocean trenches	2
	for a sea floor map	any number
	the "what, where, when, why" of hot water sea-vents	4
	the "who, what, where, when" of any of the following people: Matthew Fontaine Maury, Harry Hammond Hess, William Maurice Ewing	4

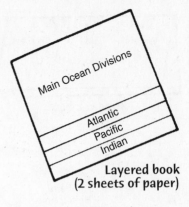

Layered book
(2 sheets of paper)

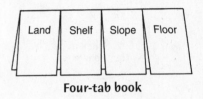

Four-tab book

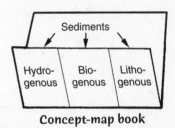

Concept-map book

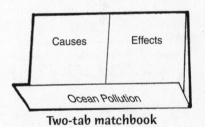

Two-tab matchbook

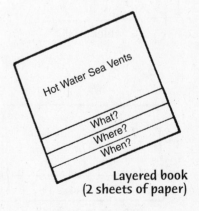

Layered book
(2 sheets of paper)

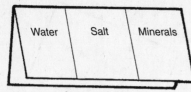

Three-tab book

Water | Salt | Minerals

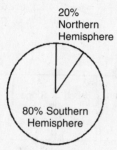

20% Northern Hemisphere
80% Southern Hemisphere

Circle graph

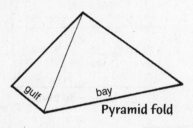

gulf | bay

Pyramid fold

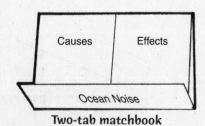

Ocean	Surface Area	Depth	Average Temp.
A			
P			
I			

Folded table

Causes | Effects
Ocean Noise

Two-tab matchbook

Oceanography

Skill	Activity Suggestion	Foldable Parts
compare and contrast	the ocean biome and another biome	2
	the oceans by depth	2
	the oceans by surface area	2
	the oceans by number of islands and volcanoes	2
	seas, gulfs, and bays	3
debate	calling our planet "Earth" instead of "Ocean"	2
	the question "Who owns the ocean?"	2
	the current state of countries owning the ocean shelf along coastal borders	2
	the world's oceans containing 97% of the Earth's water	2
	farming ocean plankton to supplement the world's food supply	2
describe	which ocean has the most volcanoes and why	2
diagram	the Atlantic, Pacific, and Indian oceans on a map	3
explain	oceanography as the word "ocean" combined with the word "geography"	2
	why oceans are always depicted as blue or green	1
	why some people say there are four oceans or more	1
	water composition, including water, salt, and gases	3
graph	the makeup of the world's water (97% salt water, 2% frozen water, 1% liquid freshwater)	3
	the comparison of oceans in the northern and southern hemispheres (80% southern, 20% northern)	2
	ocean water percentages (96% pure water, 3% salt, 1% other)	3
	the elements that comprise 99% of sea salt, including chlorine, sodium, magnesium, calcium, potassium, and sulfur	6
identify	major ocean resources, possibly including food, energy, minerals, medicines, and oil	any number
illustrate	the water cycle, including evaporation, condensation, and precipitation	3
invent	methods for desalinating ocean water	any number
list	advantages and disadvantages of dividing the ocean into named regions	2
make a timeline	of the ocean's geologic changes	any number
outline	the effect of global warming on the ocean's levels	any number
question	create a "know?-like to know?-learned?" about Earth's oceans	3
research	changes in the ocean's shape through geologic time	any number
	the ocean's effect on climate and weather	2
	stories, legends, and myths about the ocean	any number
	the "who, what, where, when" of Vagn Walfrid Ekman	4
show cause and effect	of ocean pollution	2
	of ocean noise pollution	2

Plate Tectonics

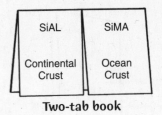

Two-tab book

Skill	Activity Suggestion	Foldable Parts
compare and contrast	continental crust and ocean crust	2
define	Mohorovicic discontinuity	1
diagram	Earth's crust, including continental and ocean crust	2
	Earth's major plates on a world map	any number
	parts of Earth, including the core, mantle, and crust	3
explain	three types of plate boundaries, including divergent, convergent, and transform	3
	how convection currents can result in plate movement	1
	relationship between fault lines and earthquakes	2
identify	rock folds, including anticlines and synclines	2
illustrate	plate movement, including how they move apart, together, and alongside each other	3
	a convection current inside Earth, including how heated less dense matter rises from deep inside Earth, this matter is cooled near Earth's surface, and then cooler, denser matter sinks	3
make a model	of an Earth cross section, including inner core, outer core, mantle, and crust	4
make a timeline	outlining the development of Continental Drift and plate tectonics	any number
	illustrating the movement of Earth's plates during the Paleozoic, Mesozoic, and Cenozoic Eras	any number
prove	the Atlantic Ocean is expanding and the Pacific is shrinking	1
question	create a "know?-like to know?-learned?" about plate tectonics	3
research	past and present views of plate tectonics	2
	the following: 1) Pangaea and Panthalassa and 2) Gondwanaland and Laurasia	2
	how scientists investigate the inside of Earth	any number
	evidence of current plate movement	any number
	ridges and trenches	2
	the deepest holes drilled by humans	any number
	information on uniform magnetic bands detected on both sides of ocean ridges and find out how they help prove seafloor spreading	any number
	the "what, when, where, why/how" of Glomar Challenger	4
	the "who, what, where, when" of any of the following people: Jason Morgan and D.P. McKenzie; Bryan L. Isacks, Jack E. Oliver, and Lynn R. Sykes; Alfred Wegener; Harold Jeffreys; Harry H. Hess	4
show cause and effect	of subduction	2
	of folding and faulting	2
	of plate tectonics	2

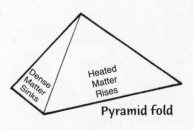

Layered book
(2 sheets of paper)

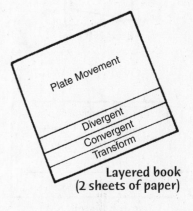

Pyramid fold

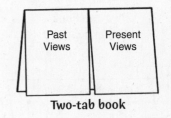

Two-tab book

Pollution: Air, Land, and Water

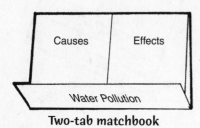

Three-tab book

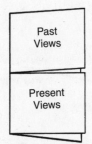

Two-tab matchbook

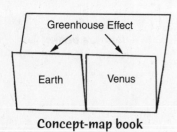

Two-tab book (vertical)

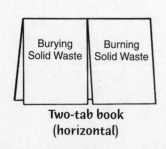

Concept-map book

Skill	Activity Suggestion	Foldable Parts
chart	ways in which water can become polluted, including petroleum products, sewage, chemicals, and metals	any number
compare and contrast	pollution that dirties the land, water, and air and pollution that reduces the quality of life, such as noise pollution	2
	point-source and nonpoint-source pollution	2
	outdoor and indoor air pollution	2
	greenhouse effect on Earth and on Venus	2
	open dumps and landfills	2
debate	using pesticides and fertilizers	2
	global warming	2
	burying solid waste versus burning it	2
define	environmental pollution	1
	smog	1
describe	how water pollution interrupts the natural cleansing processes that occur in water	1
	a solid waste disposal site	1
diagram	how pollution can affect an entire ecosystem	any number
	the greenhouse effect	any number
explain	how pollution can be reduced without reducing the quality of life on Earth	1
	the formation of acid rain	1
	why noise is a pollutant on land and in the oceans	1
graph	natural elements composing the atmosphere, including nitrogen, oxygen, argon, and others	any number
list	examples of particulates that are and are not found naturally in the atmosphere	2
	human activities that pollute soil	any number
	ways to control pollution	any number
make a timeline	of positive and negative environmental events	2
make a Venn diagram	labeled *air pollution*, *land pollution*, and *water pollution*	3
question	create a "know?-like to know?-learned?" about pollution	3
record	local news reports on ozone amounts	any number
research	the latest information on global warming	any number
	oil spills and clean-up efforts	any number
	how water pollution can lead to diseases like cholera and dysentery	any number
	what makes healthy, fertile soil	1
	the disposal of hazardous waste	1
	ways in which local, state, and national governments try to control pollution	3
	the "what, where, when, how" of radon	4
show cause and effect	of automobile use and air pollution	2
	of air pollution and respiratory problems	2
	of chlorofluorocarbons	2
	of thermal pollution	2

Rocks

Skill	Activity Suggestion	Foldable Parts
chart	examples of igneous rocks, including basalt, granite, and pumice	any number
	examples of metamorphic rocks, including gneiss, marble, and quartzite	any number
	examples of sedimentary rocks, including shale, coal, conglomerate, flint, limestone, and sandstone	any number
compare and contrast	igneous, metamorphic, and sedimentary rock	3
	foliated and nonfoliated metamorphic rocks	2
describe	rock makeup, including mixture of minerals, volcanic glass, organic matter, and other materials	1
	contact, regional, and hydrothermal metamorphism	3
	Nicholas Steno's three 1669 principals, including superposition, original horizontality, and original lateral continuity	3
diagram	the layers of soil	any number
explain	why the rock cycle has more than one path	1
	why nearly all fossils are found in sedimentary rocks	1
graph	the eight elements that make up more than 98 percent of all rocks, including oxygen, silicon, aluminum, iron, calcium, sodium, potassium, and magnesium	8
list	the most fossil-rich sedimentary rocks, including limestone, shale, chalk, sandstone, and others	any number
make a Venn diagram	labeled *rocks, minerals,* and *both*	3
	labeled *marine sedimentary rock, terrestrial sedimentary rock,* and *both*	3
observe	the importance of "human-made rock" or concrete	any number
outline	three ways to classify igneous rock by the magma from which it formed, including basaltic, andesitic, granitic	3
question	create a "know?-like to know?-learned?" about rocks and minerals	3
research	at what depth each type of rock forms	3
	igneous rocks, including extrusive and intrusive	2
	Bowen's reaction series	any number
	pumice, obsidian, and scoria	3
	sedimentary rocks, including detrital, chemical, and organic	any number
	the "what, where, when, why/how" of the idea of uniformitarianism	4
	the "who, what, when, where" of James Hutton	4

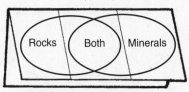

Three-tab Venn diagram

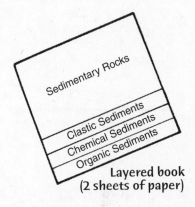

Layered book
(2 sheets of paper)

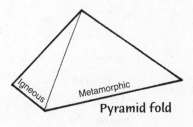

Pyramid fold

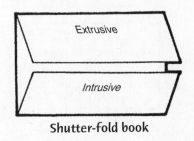

Shutter-fold book

Folded table

Volcanoes

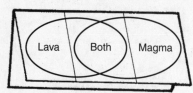

Three-tab Venn diagram

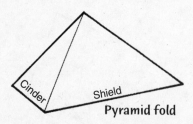

Pyramid fold

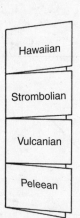

Four-tab book

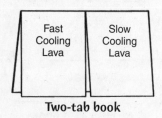

Two-tab book

Three-tab book

Skill	Activity Suggestion	Foldable Parts
compare and contrast	lava and magma	2
	different types of volcanic eruptions, including Hawaiian, Strombolian, Vulcanian, and Peleean	4
	two recent volcanic eruptions	2
	a recent and historic volcanic eruption	2
	geysers and hot springs	2
	the structure of fast and slow cooling lava	2
	a crater and a caldera	2
	ancient Thira before and after volcanic activity	2
	explosive and gradual geologic changes	2
describe	subduction zone volcanoes, rift volcanoes, and hot spot volcanoes	3
	the area before and after a historic volcanic eruption	2
determine	how the Hawaiian islands were formed	any number
diagram	the three different types of volcanoes	3
	subduction zones, rifts and hot spot volcanoes on a map	3
	active volcanoes worldwide on a map	any number
	the cross-section of a volcano	any number
	the Ring of Fire and explain its location on a map	any number
explain	the relationship between Earth's plates and volcanic activity	2
	the formation and use of pumice	2
illustrate	classification of volcanic activity, including active, intermittent, dormant, and extinct	4
	the four types of volcanic eruptions	4
make a model	of a specific volcano, possibly Mt. St. Helens or Pinatubo	any number
make a table	pertaining to volcanoes and eruptions	any number
make a timeline	of major volcanic eruptions worldwide	any number
question	create a "know?-like to know?-learned?" about volcanoes	3
research	the three main volcanic emissions, including lava, rock fragments, and gas	any number
	ocean volcanoes, including those found in the Pacific Ocean, Atlantic Ocean, and Indian Ocean	any number
	past and present volcanic activity on Iceland and Hawaii and predict future activity	3
	the "who, what, when, where" of Pliny the Younger or Nicholas Desmarest	4
sequence	events of a modern volcanic eruption, possibly Mt. St. Helens or Pinatubo	any number
show cause and effect	of Kilauea's past and recent eruptions	2
	of volcanic activity and climate changes	2
sort	volcanoes into volcano groups, including shield, cinder, and composite	3

Water

Skill	Activity Suggestion	Foldable Parts
compare and contrast	surface water and groundwater	2
	adhesion and cohesion	2
demonstrate	frozen water is less dense than liquid water	2
describe	steps for extracting freshwater from salt water	any number
design an experiment	to show the density of freshwater and salt water	any number
	to examine the properties of water, possibly including adhesion, cohesion, capillary action, surface tension, and solvency	any number
determine	what mercury and water have in common	2
diagram	the water cycle, including evaporation, condensation, and precipitation	3
discuss	the statement "With few exceptions, the water that is now on Earth has always been here." (An exception being water brought by comets and asteroids entering Earth's atmosphere.)	1
explain	why the water cycle is also called the hydrologic cycle	1
	how the water cycle is powered by solar energy	1
	several sources of water in the atmosphere, including evaporation from ocean and freshwater surfaces, human perspiration, and plant transpiration	any number
graph	the percentages of water in living organisms, possibly including jellyfish, frogs, human babies, and dogs	any number
	human blood contents, including how water makes up about 80 percent of human blood	any number
identify	the hydrosphere as all bodies of water, ice, and water in atmosphere	3
justify	the statement "Earth is called the water planet."	1
	the statement "Water is the universal solvent."	1
list	ways the human body uses water, including tears, lymph fluid, saliva, blood, urine, and sweat	any number
	advantages and disadvantages of gravity moving water	2
make a Venn diagram	labeled *freshwater*, *brackish water*, and *salt water*	3
prove	the statement "Water is found on Earth in all three states of matter at the same time."	1
question	create a "know?-like to know?-learned?" about water	3
research	methods for purifying freshwater	any number
	ways plants and animals have adapted to survive with little water	any number
	the "who, what, when, where" of Henry Cavendish or Robert Elmer Horton	4
show cause and effect	of an ocean of water covering nearly three fourths of Earth's surface	2
	of water pressure	2

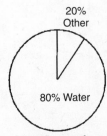

Two-tab book (vertical)

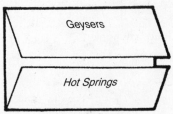

Circle graph: Human Blood Content

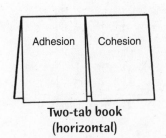

Shutter-fold book

Two-tab book (horizontal)

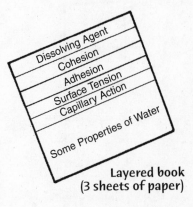

Layered book (3 sheets of paper)

Weather

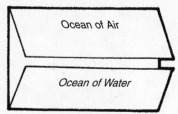

Shutter-fold book

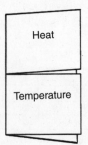

Two-tab book

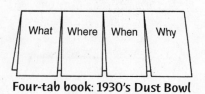

Four-tab book: 1930's Dust Bowl

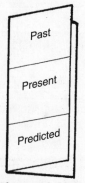

Three-tab book

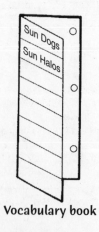

Vocabulary book

Skill	Activity Suggestion	Foldable Parts
chart	ways in which weather affects life	any number
	common weather myths and corresponding science facts	2
compare and contrast	Earth's ocean of air and its ocean of water	2
	weather and climate	2
	predicted and actual weather conditions	2
	heat and temperature	2
describe	the events before, during, and after a weather disaster in your community, possibly including a blizzard, flood, windstorm, or ice storm	3
diagram	the greenhouse effect	any number
explain	the effects of weather on commercial planes, space-shuttle launches, military operations, commerce, or others	any number
graph	weather data by weeks and months	any number
illustrate	a convection current and explain how it influences weather	any number
	weather map symbols	any number
justify	money spent on weather forecasting	any number
make a table	to record daily and weekly weather, possibly including temperature, wind, cloud cover, sunrise and sunset, and precipitation	any number
make a timeline	on the history of meteorology	any number
	illustrating the history of specific tools used for measuring weather, possibly including rain gauge, wind vane, or barometer	any number
question	create a "know?-like to know?-learned?" about weather	3
research	the importance of satellites to weather forecasting	any number
	weather myths and folklore	any number
	the layers of Earth's atmosphere as they relate to weather, including information about the troposphere	any number
	unusual weather phenomena, possibly including sun dogs and sun or moon halos	any number
	the effect of El Nino on ocean life	any number
	weather Internet sites that provide worldwide forecasts	any number
	weather reports for three cities for a given time	3
	the "what, where, when, why" of the Dust Bowl during the 1930s	4
	the "who, what, where, when" of James Glaisher or James Pollard Espy	4
sequence	the events of a weather forecast	any number
show cause and effect	of Sun's energy to Earth's weather	2
	of weather on life within any given ecosystem	any number
	of El Nino	any number
	of increasing CO_2 in the atmosphere	2
	of the greenhouse effect	2

Weather: Clouds

Skill	Activity Suggestion	Foldable Parts
chart	the conditions needed for cloud formation	any number
	your own cloud cover classification system (for example: clear, scattered, broken, overcast)	any number
classify	types of clouds observed over a period of time	any number
compare and contrast	clouds that do and do not produce rain	2
define	clouds as water vapor that has condensed into visible moisture	1
describe	cloud formation at these different levels: low-altitude clouds, middle-altitude clouds, high-altitude clouds	3
	the relationship between fog and visibility	2
explain	how clouds can be at more than one height	1
	cloud colors	1
graph	the number of days with and without a particular weather phenomenon such as smog or fog	any number
illustrate	levels of clouds, including low, middle, and high clouds	3
make a chart	for cloud identification	any number
	oktas used to measure cloud cover	any number
make a mobile	of clouds at different levels	any number
make a timeline	for the history of lighthouses	any number
make a Venn diagram	labeled *minute water droplets, ice crystals,* and *both*	3
	labeled *vapor trails, clouds,* and *both*	3
observe	cloud shapes and movement	2
question	create a "know?-like to know?-learned?" about clouds	3
research	the classification of clouds, including cirrus, cirrostratus, cirrocumulus, altocumulus, stratocumulus, cumulus, stratus, nimbostratus, altostratus	9
	ways in which clouds form, including convection, lifting, and frontal activity	3
	kinds of fog, including advection fog, frontal fog, radiation fog, and upslope fog	4
	cloud seeding in the past and present	2
	the "who, what, where, when" of Luke Howard	4
show cause and effect	of particulates in the air, possibly including dust, volcanic smoke, chemical wastes, pollen, particulates of salt from ocean spray, and crashing waves	2
	of fog	2
summarize	how smog forms	1

Three-tab book

Layered book (5 sheets of paper)

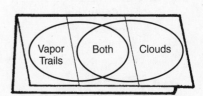

Bound-book journal

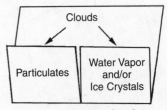

Three-tab Venn diagram

Concept-map book

Weather: Precipitation

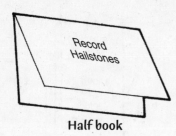

Half book

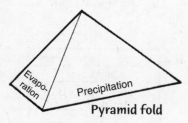

Pyramid fold

Wet Snow

Dry Snow

Two-tab book

Skill	Activity Suggestion	Foldable Parts
compare and contrast	actual raindrop shape and perceived shape	2
	rainfall amounts, including trace, light, moderate, and heavy rain	4
	regions of Earth that receive high and low levels of precipitation	2
	dry snow and wet snow	2
	hail and sleet	2
describe	the formation of hailstones	1
design	six-sided paper snow crystals	any number
diagram	the water cycle, including evaporation, condensation, and precipitation	3
	a rainbow	any number
graph	the recorded sizes of hailstones	any number
	amounts of precipitation over a period of time	any number
illustrate	the cause of rain drop's shape and size	2
	the cross section of a hailstone	any number
make a model	of snow crystals, including platelike and columnar patterns	2
question	create a "know?-like to know?-learned?" about precipitation	3
research	how the study of tree rings can help determine past rainfall amounts	1
	the "who, what, when, where" of Rene Descartes (with regards to rainbows) or To Harold Percival Bergeron	4
sequence	the events in the formation of frost	any number
show cause and effect	of a rain shadow	2

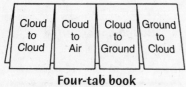

Four-tab book (horizontal)

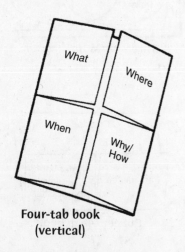

Four-tab book (vertical)

Weather: Thunder and Lightning

Skill	Activity Suggestion	Foldable Parts
compare and contrast	different types of lightning, including cloud-to-cloud, cloud-to-air, cloud-to-ground, ground-to-cloud	4
debate	the statement "Lightning will never be harnessed for energy."	2
define	thunder and lightning	2
explain	what happens inside a thunderstorm	1
graph	data concerning the percentage of lightning bolts that actually strike Earth	any number
illustrate	forms of lightning, including forked, streak, ribbon, bead, sheet, or ball lightning	6
question	create a "know?-like to know?-learned?" about thunder and lightning	3
research	regions that receive the most lightning strikes	any number
	the "who, what, when, where" of Benjamin Franklin	4
write	a lightning safety brochure	any number

Weather: Wind

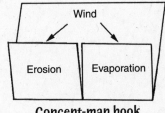

Folded table

Skill	Activity Suggestion	Foldable Parts
chart	Beaufort's wind scale	17
compare and contrast	several different wind scales, possibly including Beaufort, Saffir-Simpson Scale, Fujita Scale	any number
	windward and leeward	2
debate	pros and cons of using wind turbines	2
describe	the wind as a renewable energy source	1
	air masses	2
design	your own wind measurement scale	any number
	a wind vane and describe how it works	any number
	wind chimes	any number
locate	Earth's primary wind belts on a globe	6
make a table	to record direction and velocity of wind for a given time	any number
	of wind information, possibly including name, location, hot or cold, and season	any number
make a timeline	showing the use of wind-generated energy	any number
observe	wind socks	any number
	the wind as a force that causes movement, including flags, sails, and windmills	1
question	create a "know?-like to know?-learned?" about wind	3
research	instruments used to measure wind speed	any number
	the history of wind chimes	any number
	air mass types, including Polar Continental, Polar Maritime, Tropical Continental, and Tropical Maritime	4
	fronts, including cold front, warm front, and stationary front	3
	wind names around the world, possibly including Bora, Cat's paw, Chinook, Fohn, Mistral, El Norte, Northwester, Santa Ana, Southeaster, Tehuantepecer	any number
	how gliders and hot air balloons work	1
	current information on wind as an energy source	any number
	the "who, what, when, where" of any of the following people: Hendrik Buy Ballot, Gustave-Gaspard Coriolis, William Dampier, William Ferrel, George Hadley	4
show cause and effect	of wind	2
	of wind and erosion	2
	of wind and evaporation	2
	of trade winds to the world's climate	2

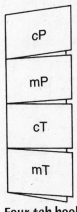

Concept-map book

Four-tab book

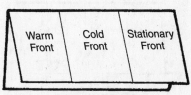

Three-tab book

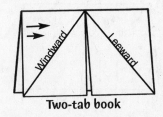

Two-tab book

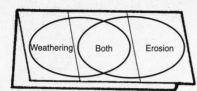
Three-tab Venn diagram

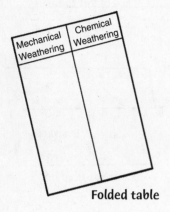
Folded table

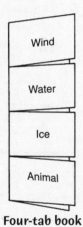
Four-tab book

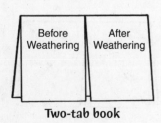
Two-tab matchbook

Before Weathering | After Weathering

Two-tab book

Weathering and Soil

Skill	Activity Suggestion	Foldable Parts
chart	examples of mechanical weathering, including exfoliation, plant roots, burrowing animals, freezing water in rock cracks, sandpaper effect of particles in wind	any number
	examples of chemical weathering, including carbonic acid, lichens, acids formed by decaying organic matter, oxygen in the air combining with minerals	any number
compare and contrast	weathering and erosion	2
	mechanical and chemical weathering	2
	how effective different kinds of plants are at preventing erosion and holding soil, including trees, grass, and legumes	2
debate	the pros and cons of trying to prevent erosion	2
define	pedologist and polypedons	2
describe	weathering as deterioration or breaking of parent rock into smaller pieces	1
	a land formation before and after weathering	2
	soil contents	any number
	how soil formation depends on the environment, including time, climate, parent rock, surface of land, and living organisms in an area	any number
determine	agents of weathering, including ice, water, acids, plant roots, temperature changes	any number
explain	how soils are formed and destroyed	2
	nutrients in soil	1
list	soil contents, including minerals, organic matter, air, and water	4
observe	the effects of wind on materials	any number
	soil characteristics, including color, composition, and location	3
question	create a "know?-like to know?-learned?" about weathering and soil	3
research	the changes in Earth's surface, including weathering, erosion, mass movements, changes in crust	4
	what flowing or dripping water can do to solid rock	any number
	sands, silts, and clays	3
	common minerals that form sands and silts, including quartz and feldspars	2
	minerals that form clays, including illite, kaolinite, smectite, and vermiculite	4
	soil organisms	any number
	farming techniques that prevent erosion of top soil	any number
	the "who, what, when, where" of John Welsey Powell	4
show cause and effect	of droughts on weathering and erosion	2

Foldables for Life Science/Biology

The following science topics are covered in this section:

Animals

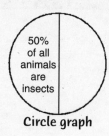

50%
of all
animals
are
insects

Circle graph

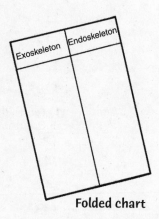

Exoskeleton | Endoskeleton

Folded chart

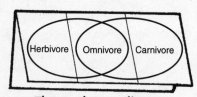

Young with Parental Care | Young without Parental Care

Compare and Contrast

Two-tab matchbook

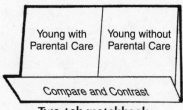

Herbivore | Omnivore | Carnivore

Three-tab Venn diagram

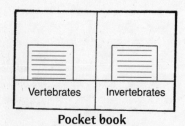

Vertebrates | Invertebrates

Pocket book

Skill	Activity Suggestion	Foldable Parts
chart	the phyla of the animal kingdom and list examples	any number
	animals by terrestrial or aquatic habitat	2
	animals common to each continent	7
compare and contrast	vertebrates and invertebrates	2
	animals with endoskeletons and exoskeletons	2
	animals with one and two body openings	2
	young that do and do not receive parental care	2
describe	animals, including how they are composed of many cells, capable of voluntary movement, etc.	any number
	animals in terms of invertebrates and vertebrates	2
diagram	animal life cycles	any number
	migratory routes of selected animals on a map	any number
discuss	humankind's use of animals in the past, present, and future	3
explain	the role of animals in the web of life	1
	animal regeneration	1
	why some animals become endangered and others do not	1
group	animals by number of legs, either bipedal or quadrupedal	2
illustrate	form and function of the three basic animal body plans, including acoelomate, pseudocoelomate, and coelomate plans	3
list	examples of warm-blooded and cold-blooded species	2
	advantages and disadvantages for being endothermic and ectothermic	2
	advantages and disadvantages of sexual and asexual reproduction	2
make a Venn diagram	about animal diets labeled *carnivores, herbivores,* and *omnivores*	3
map	animals by their specific habitats	any number
observe	adaptations of animal respiration on land and in water	2
prove	the statement "About fifty percent of all known species of animals are insects."	1
question	create a "know?-like to know?-learned?" about animals	3
research	the pros and cons of internal versus external skeletons	2
	herbivores that are frugivorous (i.e., their diet is mainly fruit)	1
	carnivores that are insectivorous (i.e., their diet is mainly insect)	1
	solutions to the problem of protection from predators, possibly including camouflage, hiding, speed, armor, claws, talons, horns, fangs, playing dead, chemical defense, or ability to lose a body part	any number
	pros and cons of animals living in a community	2
	migration and explain why animals migrate	2
	the main reasons for animals becoming endangered, including loss of habitat, introduction of new species to their habitat, pollution, hunting, and human population growth within their habitat	any number
show cause and effect	of different types of animal locomotion	2
summarize	animal respiration, including taking in oxygen and giving out carbon dioxide	1

Animals: Invertebrates

Skill	Activity Suggestion	Foldable Parts
graph	the ratio of invertebrates to vertebrates (about 90 percent to 10 percent)	2
question	create a "know?-like to know?-learned?" about invertebrates	3

Phylum Rotifera

Skill	Activity Suggestion	Foldable Parts
diagram	body form and function	2
explain	why rotifera are called "wheel animals"	1
list	examples of *Brachionus calciflorus*	any number
question	create a "know?-like to know?-learned?" about rotiferan	3
research	rotiferan habitats, including lakes, streams, and oceans	3
	body shape, cilia, and average size	3
	parthenogenesis reproduction in rotifer populations	1

Phylum Ectoprocta or Bryozoa

Skill	Activity Suggestion	Foldable Parts
describe	body form and function, including tentacles clustered on the head and others	any number
diagram	body shapes and parts, including boxlike and tube-shaped	any number
explain	why they are called "moss animals"	1
illustrate	what the colonies look like	any number
list	examples of Bowing ectoproct	any number
question	create a "know?-like to know?-learned?" about ectoprocts or bryozoans	3
research	why ectoprocts live in water and usually form colonies	1

Phylum Cnidaria

Skill	Activity Suggestion	Foldable Parts
compare and contrast	sessile and free-swimming cnidarians	2
	jellyfish and hydras	2
	the lives of jellyfish that swim freely and those carried by water movement	2
create	a cnidarian identification chart	any number
describe	cnidarians' radially symmetrical bodies	1
diagram	body form and function, including polyp and medusa	2
	on a map the Great Barrier Reef and other coral reefs	any number
list	pros and cons for living alone versus living in colonies	2
make a Venn diagram	labeled *cnidarian sexual reproduction, cnidarian asexual reproduction,* and *cnidarian that reproduce both sexually and asexually*	3
question	create a "know?-like to know?-learned?" about cnidarians	3
research	a cnidarian, possibly including corals, jellyfish, hydras, sea fans, and sea anemones	1
	stinging cells	any number
	the conditions needed for and the importance of coral reefs	2

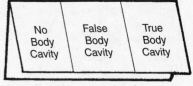

Three-tab book

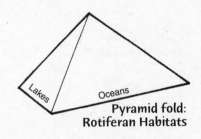

Pyramid fold:
Rotiferan Habitats

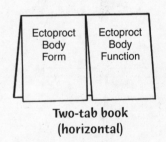

Two-tab book
(horizontal)

Two-tab book
(vertical)

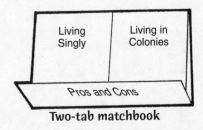

Two-tab matchbook

"There are more known species extinct than living."

Half book

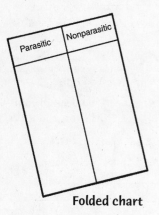

Parasitic | Nonparasitic

Folded chart

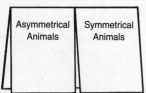

Asymmetrical Animals | Symmetrical Animals

Two-tab book (horizontal)

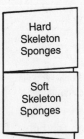

Hard Skeleton Sponges

Soft Skeleton Sponges

Two-tab book (vertical)

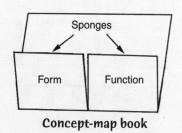

Sponges

Form | Function

Concept-map book

Phylum Brachiopoda

Skill	Activity Suggestion	Foldable Parts
compare and contrast	brachiopods that attach to surfaces and those that live in sand	2
create	a brachiopod identification chart	any number
diagram	body form and function, including two shells and a soft body	2
prove	that there are more known species of brachiopods that are extinct than living	1
question	create a "know?-like to know?-learned?" about brachiopods	3
research	brachiopods and why they are called "lamp shells"	1
	one of the thousands of extinct species	1

Phylum Acanthocephala

Skill	Activity Suggestion	Foldable Parts
compare and contrast	parasitic animals to nonparasitic animals	2
describe	an acanthocephalan's habitat	1
diagram	body form and function	any number
question	create a "know?-like to know?-learned?" about acanthocephalan	3

Phylum Porifera

Skill	Activity Suggestion	Foldable Parts
compare and contrast	asymmetrical and symmetrical animals	2
	shallow- and deep-water sponges	2
	marine and freshwater sponges	2
	types of sponge skeletons	2
create	a sponge classification chart	any number
define	"sessile" and apply the word to sponges	2
describe	filter feeders and use sponges as an example	2
diagram	sponge body form and function	2
explain	why early scientists classified sponges as plants	1
graph	sponges by size	any number
list	advantages of sponge regeneration	any number
	the pros and cons of a sessisle life	2
make a Venn diagram	labeled *sponges*, *humans*, and *both*	3
question	create a "know?-like to know?-learned?" about sponges	3
research	sponges known through fossil evidence	any number
	collar cells form and function	2
	the commercialization of sponges and its impact on the environment	2

Phylum Ctenophora

Skill	Activity Suggestion	Foldable Parts
compare and contrast	ctenophores to true jellyfish	2
describe	ctenophore habitat	1
diagram	Venus' girdle	any number
	body form and function	2
graph	size of comb jellies	any number
question	create a "know?-like to know?-learned?" about ctenophores	3
research	comb jellies (also called sea walnuts)	1
	bioluminescent ctenophores	1

Phylum Platyhelminthes

Skill	Activity Suggestion	Foldable Parts
compare and contrast	parasitic and nonparasitic species	2
	marine and freshwater species of flatworms	2
describe	planarians	any number
diagram	body form and function	2
graph	sizes of common flatworms	any number
question	create a "know?-like to know?-learned?" about platyhelminthes	3
research	flatworms, including tapeworms, flukes, and planarians	3
	flatworm reproduction	2

Phylum Nematoda

Skill	Activity Suggestion	Foldable Parts
compare and contrast	parasitic and nonparasitic roundworms	2
	the number of body openings of flatworms and roundworms	2
	flatworm and roundworm reproduction	2
describe	roundworm habitats, including soil, water, dead, and living tissue	any number
diagram	body form and function	2
explain	the advantages of having a one-way digestive tract	1
graph	sizes of roundworms	any number
question	create a "know?-like to know?-learned?" about nematodes	3
research	nematodes, including filariae, hookworms, pinworms, and trichinae	any number
	what effect nematodes can have on plants	1

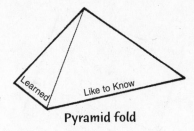

Pyramid fold

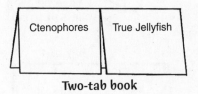

Two-tab book

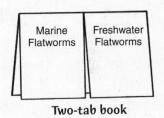

Two-tab book

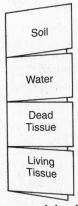

Four-tab book

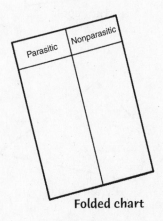

Folded chart

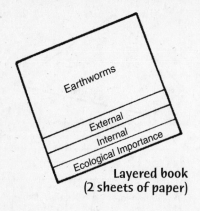

Earthworms

External
Internal
Ecological Importance

Layered book
(2 sheets of paper)

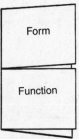

Past | Present

Medicinal Uses of Leeches

Two-tab matchbook

Form

Function

Two-tab book

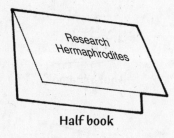

Research
Hermaphrodites

Half book

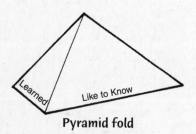

Learned | Like to Know

Pyramid fold

Phylum Nemertea

Skill	Activity Suggestion	Foldable Parts
diagram	ribbon worm body form and function	2
illustrate	a specific ribbon worm	1
list	characteristics of ribbon worms, including marine, long proboscis, and carnivorous	any number
question	create a "know?-like to know?-learned?" about nemertean	3
research	ribbon worms or proboscis worms	1

Phylum Annelida

Skill	Activity Suggestion	Foldable Parts
apply	the term "hermaphrodite" to earthworms	1
compare and contrast	parasitic and nonparasitic leeches	2
create	an annelid identification chart	any number
debate	the use of earthworms to make flour or as a dietary supplement	2
design an experiment	to show that earthworms aerate the soil	any number
diagram	an earthworm's body parts, possibly including annuli, setae or bristles, and digestive tube	any number
	body form and function	2
explain	the past, present, and future importance of earthworms	3
	why earthworms cannot live in waterlogged soil	1
question	create a "know?-like to know?-learned?" about annelids	3
research	two segmented worms,	2
	leeches, including size, color, and diet	any number
	the historic and current importance of medicinal leeches	2
	leeches being used in microsurgery	1

Phylum Chaetognatha

Skill	Activity Suggestion	Foldable Parts
diagram	body form and function	2
graph	average sizes	any number
question	create a "know?-like to know?-learned?" about arrow worms	3
research	arrow worms' diet, habitat, locomotion, and reproduction	3
	habitat	any number

Phylum Arthropoda

Skill	Activity Suggestion	Foldable Parts
chart	characteristics, including jointed legs, segmented bodies, and exoskeletons	any number
compare and contrast	arthropods with thin exoskeletons and those that have thick exoskeletons	2
	arthropods to segmented worms	2
debate	the statement "Arthropods are nature's most successful group of organisms."	2
diagram	body form and function	2
graph	major arthropod classes (insects 88%, arachnids 7%, crustaceans 3%, centipedes and millipedes 1%, others 1%)	5
	how many animals are in the phylum Arthropoda compared to all other (75%)	2
make a Venn diagram	labeled *arthropods with compound eyes, arthropods with simple eyes,* and *both*	3
question	create a "know?-like to know?-learned?" about arthropods	3
research	four major groups of arthropods, including insects, crustaceans, arachnids, and centipedes and millipedes	4
	chitin and exoskeletons	2

Phylum Arthropoda: Crustaceans

Skill	Activity Suggestion	Foldable Parts
compare and contrast	beneficial and harmful crustaceans	2
create	a crustacean identification chart	any number
define	regeneration as it relates to crustaceans	1
diagram	body parts, including head, thorax, and abdomen	3
	body form and function	2
explain	why and how some crustaceans can voluntarily lose a leg or claw to escape a predator	1
graph	examples of crustacean body sizes	any number
list	advantages and disadvantages of molting	2
question	create a "know?-like to know?-learned?" about crustaceans	3
research	crustaceans, possibly including shrimp, crabs, lobster, crayfish, barnacles, water fleas, wood lice, and cepopods	any number
	molting and regeneration	2
	commercial importance of crustaceans	1
	how baleen whales depend on krill	1
	the life cycle of barnacles	any number
	land and aquatic wood lice	2
write	a crustacean recipe book	any number

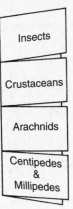

Four-tab book

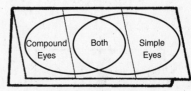

Three-tab Venn diagram

Two-tab book

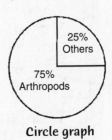

Circle graph

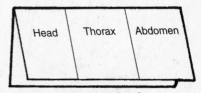

Three-tab book

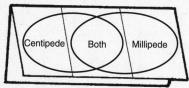
Three-tab Venn diagram

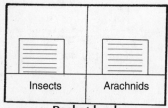
Pocket book

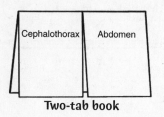
Two-tab book

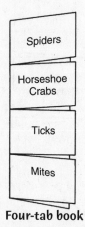
Four-tab book

Shutter-fold book

Phylum Arthropoda: Centipedes and Millipedes

Skill	Activity Suggestion	Foldable Parts
compare and contrast	centipedes and millipedes	2
create	a centipede and millipede identification chart	any number
diagram	body form and function	2
make a table	of information on centipedes and millipedes, including length, leg number, diet, habitat, and reproduction	any number
question	create a "know?-like to know?-learned?" about centipedes and millipedes	3
research	the poisonous jaws or fangs of a centipede	1

Phylum Arthropoda: Arachnids

Skill	Activity Suggestion	Foldable Parts
compare and contrast	arachnids and insects	2
create	an arachnid identification chart	any number
describe	arachnid legs	1
	how hummingbirds use spider webs to build their nests	1
	how jumping spiders move and catch prey	1
design an experiment	to determine the strength of a spider web	any number
diagram	arachnid body parts, including cephalothorax and abdomen	2
	body form and function	2
explain	how spiders consume liquid food	1
	why all spiders are poisonous but few are dangerous to humans	1
graph	sizes of scorpions	any number
	sizes of spiders	any number
illustrate	size and shape of egg cases in spider webs	any number
list	examples of spiders that are harmful and beneficial	any number
observe	arachnid movement	any number
	spider webs and sketch an example	any number
prove	the statement "Daddy-long legs are not spiders."	1
question	create a "know?-like to know?-learned?" about arachnids	3
research	four examples of arachnids, including mites, ticks, spiders, and horseshoe crabs	4
	one species of arachnid in terms of diet, size, habitat, length of life	4
	exoskeleton	1
	Lyme disease	1
	black widows and brown recluse spiders	2
	orb and net webs	2
	the "what, where, when, how" of *Argyroneta aquatica* or Rocky Mountain spotted fever	4
	the "who, what, where, when" of Dr. Thomas Muffet	4

Phylum Arthropoda: Insects

Skill	Activity Suggestion	Foldable Parts
chart	characteristics of insects, possibly including three pairs of jointed legs, three body parts, exoskeleton, one or two pairs of wings	any number
collect	dead insects, observe, identify, and label	any number
compare and contrast	chewing insects and sucking insects	2
	insects with two and four wings	2
	complete and incomplete metamorphosis	2
create	an insect identification chart	any number
debate	the pros and cons of using pesticides to kill insects	2
describe	insect legs	1
	how insects can be transferred from one habitat to another	1
diagram	insect body parts, including head, thorax, and abdomen	3
	body form and function	2
explain	why insects are such successful animals	1
graph	the percent of insects that go through complete and incomplete metamorphosis	2
	insects by length, wingspans, antennae, etc.	any number
identify	caterpillars, maggots, grubs, and wrigglers as insect larvae	1
illustrate	and describe several insect habitats	any number
infer	as to why insects have remained relatively small in size	1
list	positive and negative outcomes of collecting insects for money and sport	2
	examples of nocturnal and diurnal insects	2
make a table	on different insects, possibly including size, diet, habitat, and life span	any number
make a Venn diagram	labeled *insects, arachnids,* and *both*	3
	labeled *insects, bugs,* and *both*	3
observe	insect movement	any number
prove	the statement "Pillbugs are not insects."	1
question	create a "know?-like to know?-learned?" about insects	3
research	exoskeleton, chitin, molting	3
	insects with two wings	any number
	insects with four wings	any number
	pheromones	1
	honeybees, including workers, drones, and queens	3
	social insects	any number
	brine flies and explain why they are so unusual	2
	why a ladybug is not a bug	1
	plants that attract specific insects, such as butterflies	1
	the history of insect collecting	any number
	government insect collection programs, including killer bees, harmful fruit flies, mosquitoes, and fire ants	any number
	what is known about prehistoric insects based upon fossils	any number
	insect specialization	1

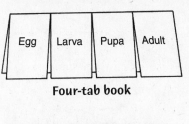

Four-tab book

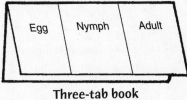

Three-tab book

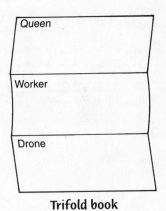

Trifold book

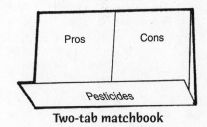

Two-tab matchbook

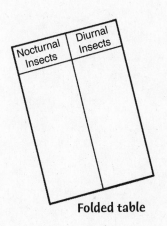

Folded table

Phylum Echinodermata

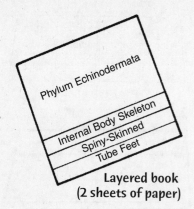

Layered book
(2 sheets of paper)

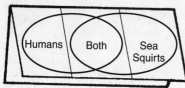

Three-tab Venn diagram

Skill	Activity Suggestion	Foldable Parts
compare and contrast	radial symmetry and bilateral symmetry	2
	the tube feet of echinoderms to suction cups	2
create	an echinoderm identification chart	any number
describe	how sea stars feed on mollusks such as oysters and clams	1
diagram	body parts, including internal body skeleton, spiny skin, and tube feet	3
	body form and function	2
explain	why starfish are not fish	1
make a table	of sea star species, including sizes, shapes, number of arms, color, and habitat	any number
observe	the internal skeleton of an echinoderm	1
prove	the statement "This phylum is the only phylum with marine animals."	1
question	create a "know?-like to know?-learned?" about echinoderms	3
research	several echinoderms, including brittle stars, sand dollars, sea urchins, sea cucumbers, sea stars	any number
	the water-vascular system found in all echinoderms	1
	defense mechanisms for different echinoderms	any number
	sea urchins, possibly including size, movement, predators, and habitat	any number

Phylum Mollusks

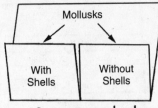

Concept-map book

Skill	Activity Suggestion	Foldable Parts
compare and contrast	mollusks with and without outside shells	2
	land, freshwater, and saltwater snails	3
	bivalves and univalves	2
	an octopus and a squid	2
	octopus, squid, cuttlefish, and nautilus	4
	paper nautilus and chambered nautilus	2
create	a mollusk identification chart	any number
define	cephalopod	1
diagram	parts of a univalve shell and a bivalve shell	2
	body form and function	2
	outer, middle, and inner layers of shells	3
imagine	how prehistoric people might have used shells for tools	any number
make a table	on the classes of mollusks	any number
	of tooth shell information, including size, color, and habitat	any number
predict	how snails and slugs might cause crop damage	1
prove	the statement "This phylum is the largest group of water animals"	1
question	create a "know?-like to know?-learned?" about mollusks	3
research	several mollusks, including clams, mussels, octopuses, oysters, snails, squids	any number
	different kinds of gastropods	any number
	different kinds of bivalves	any number
	giant squids	1
	how some mollusks produce pearls	1

Mollusks

Clams
Mussels
Octopuses
Snails
Oysters
Squids

**Layered book
(4 sheets of paper)**

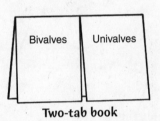

Two-tab book

Animals Vertebrates

Skill	Activity Suggestion	Foldable Parts
chart	the seven classes of vertebrates, including three classes of fish, amphibians, reptiles, birds, and mammals	7
	vertebrates that are endotherms and ectotherms	2
describe	what all chordates have in common (for example, at some point during their life, they all have notochords, a dorsal hollow nerve cord, a postanal tail, and gill slits)	3
	the statement "Vertebrates have two pair of limbs."	1
diagram	a cross-section of a vertebrae enclosing the dorsal nerve cord	1
explain	why all vertebrates are members of the phylum Chordata	1
	traces of gills that can be seen in human embryos	1
list	vertebrates of land, freshwater, marine, and air	4
	vertebrates that are ectotherms and endotherms	2
make a Venn diagram	labeled *humans, sea squirts,* and *both*	3
observe	how vertebrates usually have a head and a body trunk	2
outline	the purposes of an endoskeleton	any number
prove	that vertebrates are bilaterally symmetrical	1
question	create a "know?-like to know?-learned?" about chordates	3
research	the three subphylum of Chordata, including vertebrates, tunicates, and lancelets	3

Seven Classes of Vertebrates
Jawless Fish
Cartilaginous Fish
Bony Fish
Amphibians
Reptiles
Birds
Mammals

**Layered book
(4 sheets of paper)**

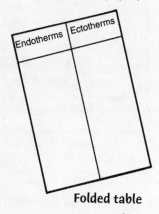

Folded table

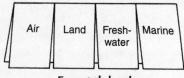

**Layered book
(2 sheets of paper)**

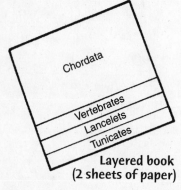

Four-tab book

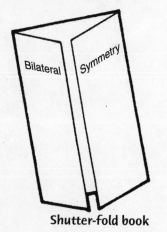

Shutter-fold book

Phylum Chordata: Fish

Skill	Activity Suggestion	Foldable Parts
chart	fish by their diets	any number
compare and contrast	bony and cartilaginous fish	2
	modern and primitive bony fish	2
	cold blooded fish to warm blooded animals	2
compile	a fish cookbook and include nutritional information	any number
create	a shark identification chart	any number
describe	cartilaginous fish, including cartilage, rough skin, unequally divided tail, and gills	any number
	bony fish, including bone skeleton, scales or plates, equally divided tail, and gills	any number
	paired fins, including pectoral and pelvic	2
diagram	a fish food chain or food web	any number
	a fish and its fins, including anal, dorsal, and caudal	3
	the Comoro Islands, home of the coelacanth, on a map	1
explain	how a fish breathes under water, including gill slits, chamber, and cover	3
	an air bladder and buoyancy	2
	why the Devonian Period of the Paleozoic Era is called the "Age of Fishes"	1
graph	smallest to largest fish	any number
	modern bony fish (95%), primitive bony fish (1%), cartilaginous fish (3%)	3
identify	fish habitats, including freshwater, brackish water, and saltwater environments	3
illustrate	two different kinds of scales, including ctenoid and cycloid	2
	rayed fins, including soft and spiny	2
make a Venn diagram	labeled *jawed fish, jawless fish,* and *both*	3
observe	aquarium fish and research their therapeutic uses	any number
outline	the importance of fish to humankind as documented through archaeological discoveries	any number
question	create a "know?-like to know?-learned?" about fish	3
relate	fish body forms to habitat and life functions	1
research	the classes of fish, including jawless, cartilaginous, and bony	3
	lampreys and hagfish	2
	"fish" that are not really fish, including jellyfish and shellfish	any number
	types of scales, including ganoid scales and placoid scales	2
	lung fish and estivation	1
	pros and cons of internal and external fertilization	2
	spawning seasons and spawning grounds	2
	how fish are used commercially	any number
	fishing as a sport	1
	how fish reproduce	any number
	current commercial fishing methods	any number
	the discovery of the "extinct" coelacanth	1

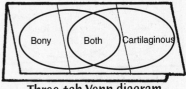

Three-tab Venn diagram

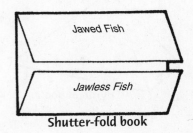

Shutter-fold book

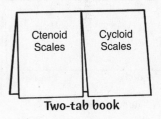

Two-tab book

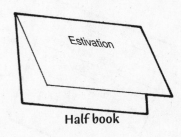

Half book

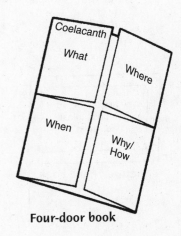

Four-door book

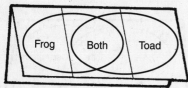

Three-tab Venn diagram

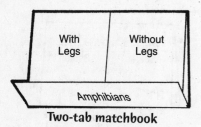

Pyramid book

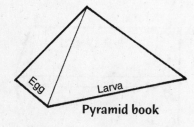

Two-tab matchbook

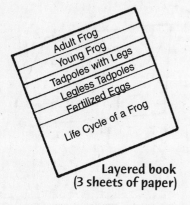

**Layered book
(3 sheets of paper)**

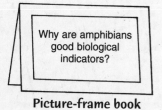

Picture-frame book

Phylum Chordata: Amphibians

Skill	Activity Suggestion	Foldable Parts
chart	information on different kinds of amphibians, possibly including diet, size, color, habitat, and reproduction	any number
compare and contrast	true toads and true frogs	2
	amphibians with and without tails	2
	amphibians with and without legs	2
	the skin of an amphibian and a fish	2
	amphibian eggs and reptile or bird eggs	2
create	a frog or toad identification chart	any number
describe	amphibian metamorphosis from egg to larvae to adult	3
diagram	examples of amphibians living on every continent except Antarctica on a map	6
explain	amphibians as ectotherms	2
	why amphibian eggs, unlike bird eggs, do not develop and hatch in a given number of days	1
hypothesize	why amphibians are good biological indicators	1
illustrate	the life cycle of a frog or toad, including fertilized eggs, legless tadpoles, tadpoles with legs, young frogs, and adults	5
	the life cycle of a salamander	any number
list	four characteristics of amphibians, including that it begins life in water, moist skin, four limbs, webbed feet, cold-blooded	4
make a Venn diagram	labeled *frog, toad,* and *both*	3
	labeled *hibernation, estivation,* and *both*	3
observe	amphibian locomotion, noting leg size, leg movement, and distance moved	3
	sounds of amphibians around ponds or lakes	any number
question	create a "know?-like to know?-learned?" about amphibians	3
research	three groups of amphibians, including frogs and toads, salamanders, and caecilians	3
	the life of an amphibian in and out of water	2
	the importance of water in an amphibian's life cycle	1
	blue poison-arrow frog of South America	1
	fossil evidence of amphibians	1
	when amphibians were the dominant land animals on Earth	1
	bullfrogs' growth and development	2
	mud puppies and how they retain their external gills as adults	1

Phylum Chordata: Reptiles

Skill	Activity Suggestion	Foldable Parts
compare and contrast	reptiles that do and do not hibernate	2
	poisonous reptiles and nonpoisonous reptiles	2
	lizards with and without legs	2
	lizards and snakes	2
	overlapping scales and plate scales	2
	turtles and tortoises	2
	reptile eggs and bird eggs	2
create	a snake identification chart	any number
describe	reptiles, including dry skin, scales or bony plates, leathery-shelled eggs, breathe with lungs, cold-blooded	any number
	characteristics of lizards, including that they usually have four legs, long tails, moveable eyelids, and external ear openings	any number
	characteristics of snakes, including tails, no legs, no eyelids, and no ear openings	any number
	characteristics of turtles, including a shell, four legs, and short tails	any number
	characteristics of crocodilians, including four legs, webbed hind feet, scales, long snout, strong jaws	any number
diagram	on a map the habitats of different snake species	any number
	on a map crocodilian habitats	any number
explain	the importance of molting to reptiles	1
graph	life expectancy of numerous different reptiles	any number
identify	turtle habitats, including land, freshwater, and marine	3
list	reptilian methods of obtaining food	any number
	poisonous and nonpoisonous snakes found in your ecosystem	2
	pros and cons of reptiles laying their eggs on land	2
make a mobile	of prehistoric flying, swimming, and land reptiles	3
make a timeline	of the Age of Reptiles	any number
make a Venn diagram	labeled *crocodiles, alligators,* and *both*	3
question	create a "know?-like to know?-learned?" about reptiles	3
research	the four main groups of reptiles, including lizards and snakes, turtles, crocodilians, and tuatara	4
	several reptile characteristics, including size, color, diet, and habitat	any number
	reptilian defense techniques	any number
	snake scales, including composition, arrangement, and purpose	3
	poisonous snakes and nonpoisonous snakes	2
	crocodilians, including alligators, crocodiles, caymans, and gavials	4
	the tuatara	1
	what is known about prehistoric reptiles based upon fossils	1

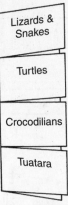

Four-tab book

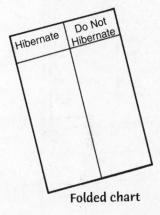

Folded chart

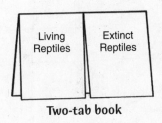

Two-tab book

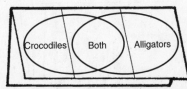

Three-tab Venn diagram

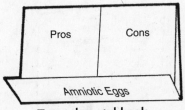

Two-tab matchbook

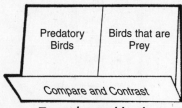

Predatory Birds | Birds that are Prey

Compare and Contrast

Two-tab matchbook

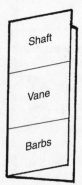

Shaft

Vane

Barbs

Three-tab book

Bird	Route	When	How Long

Folded table

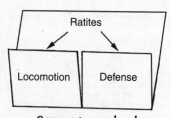

Ratites

Locomotion | Defense

Concept-map book

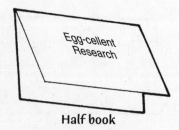

Egg-cellent Research

Half book

Phylum Chordata: Birds

Skill	Activity Suggestion	Foldable Parts
compare and contrast	the body temperature of a bird and a human	2
	birds of flight and ratites	2
	land birds and water birds	2
	physical characteristics of predatory birds and birds that are prey	2
	nocturnal and diurnal birds	2
	the feet of an ostrich to any bird of flight	2
describe	the life cycle of any bird	any number
	the anatomy of birds with and without webbed feet	2
	types of feathers, including contour and down	2
diagram	bird habitats and paths of migratory flight on a map	any number
explain	eye positions of carnivorous birds compared to eye positions of herbivorous birds	2
	how wings provide upward force for birds and airplanes	1
graph	bird record speeds (diving, running, flight)	any number
illustrate	how birds fit into different food webs	any number
	bills suited for nest building, feeding and self-defense	3
	different bird's feet	any number
	the parts of a feather, including shaft, vane, and barbs	3
	different types of nests	any number
	parts of an egg, including yolk, albumen, membranes, and shell	4
list	four characteristics of birds, possibly including warmblooded, feathers, wings, scales, hard-shelled eggs, some hollow bones, toothless, etc.	4
	examples of birds with common bird bill shapes, possibly including cone-shaped, chisel-like, broad with filters, long and pointed, scoop-like, hornbills, curved prober	any number
make a table	different species of birds, including size, color, diet, habitat, young, nests, etc.	any number
	of migration distances, routes, and time of year	3
observe	bird behaviors and note bird calls and songs	2
question	create a "know?-like to know?-learned?" about birds	3
research	two ratites, possibly including ostrich, emu, rhea, cassowary, kiwi, or penguin	2
	swimming birds	1
	bird bills, including species, shape, purpose, and diet	4
	arrangement and size of toes and shape of claws of different species of birds	any number
	what egg shells, seashells, limestone, and marble all have in common	4
	birds that do and do not build nests	2
	birds as symbols, past and present	2

Phylum Chordata: Mammals

Skill	Activity Suggestion	Foldable Parts
compare and contrast	land and aquatic mammals	2
	reproduction in mammals bearing live young and mammals that lay eggs	2
	nocturnal mammals and diurnal mammals	2
	a mammal's four-chambered heart to a reptile's heart	3
	monotremes, marsupials, and placental mammals	3
describe	mammals, including warmblooded, fur or hair, females produce milk, and live birth	4
	mammal diets, including herbivorous, carnivorous, and omnivorous	3
	what skin, hair, nails, claws, and hooves all have in common	1
diagram	the marsupial habitats, including Australia, Tasmania, New Guinea, and North America on a map	4
explain	the effect of mammals providing care for their young	1
graph	common mammal gestation periods in days	any number
identify	three basic types of teeth, including incisors, canines, and molars	3
list	endangered and threatened mammals	2
make a table	of data for 10 mammals, including size, diet, habitat, life span, and young	10
make a timeline	highlighting the Age of Mammals	any number
question	create a "know?-like to know?-learned?" about mammals	3
research	any of the mammals from the different orders	any number
	the importance of mammals to early humans	1
	ecotourism as it relates to animals	1

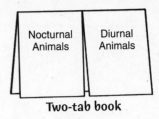

Two-tab book

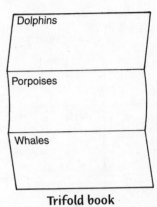

Trifold book

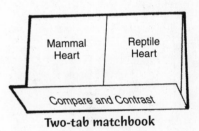

Two-tab matchbook

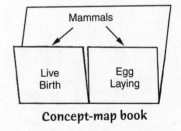

Concept-map book

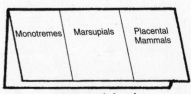

Three-tab book

Archaebacteria

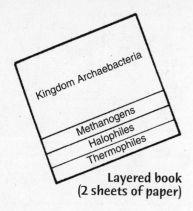

Kingdom Archaebacteria

Methanogens
Halophiles
Thermophiles

**Layered book
(2 sheets of paper)**

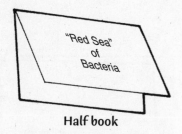

Cyano-
bacteria   Both   True
Algae

Three-tab Venn diagram

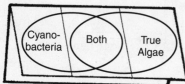

"Red Sea"
of
Bacteria

Half book

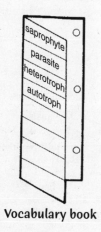

saprophyte
parasite
heterotroph
autotroph

Vocabulary book

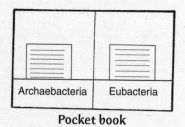

Archaebacteria   Eubacteria

Pocket book

Skill	Activity Suggestion	Foldable Parts
describe	three types of organisms in Kingdom Archaebacteria, including methanogens, halophiles, and thermophiles	3
determine	the salinity of water needed for halophiles	1
explain	why archaebacteria are called "extremophiles" and "ancient"	1
	why scientists think archaebacteria were some of the world's first living organisms	1
	why halophiles are the primary organisms found in the Dead Sea and Utah's Great Salt Lake	1
hypothesize	why halophiles need water 10 times saltier than seawater	1
list	characteristics of ancient bacteria, including anaerobic and autotrophs	any number
	environments where methanogens can be found, including sediments and soils, animal intestines, waste water, landfills, oil deposits	any number
question	create a "know?-like to know?-learned?" about archaebacteria	3
research	sea vents and thermophiles	2

Bacteria

Skill	Activity Suggestion	Foldable Parts
compare and contrast	past and present classification of bacteria	2
	beneficial bacteria and harmful bacteria	2
	aerobes and anaerobes	2
	infection and disease	2
describe	all bacteria as prokaryotes	1
	why bacteria can't reproduce by mitosis	1
diagram	a bacterium cell	any number
discuss	the statement "Bacteria has been found in every biome and region of Earth."	1
explain	how bacteria typically reproduce	1
	antibiotic resistance as evolutionary change	1
	the importance of nitrogen-fixing bacteria to agriculture	1
	the holes of Swiss cheese as they relate to bacteria	1
illustrate	the three basic shapes of bacteria, including coccus, spirillum, and bacillus	3
make a time line	on the history of pasteurization	any number
question	create a "know?-like to know?-learned?" about bacteria	3
research	why sometimes a gel-like capsule surrounds the cell wall	1
	the purpose of flagella	1
	diseases caused by bacteria, including botulism, tuberculosis, diphtheria, and tetanus	any number
	the *E. coli* bacteria	1
	the purpose of pickling and its importance to food preservation	2
	the history of canning food and investigate botulism bacteria	2
	the anaerobic bacterium *Clostridium tetani* (lockjaw)	1
	the advantages of bioremediation	any number
	antibiotic resistance	1
	Lyme disease and the bacteria that causes it	1
	past and present battles against tuberculosis and predict is future	3
	what part bacteria play in cheese production	1
	the "who, what, where, when" of Antonie van Leeuwenhoek	4

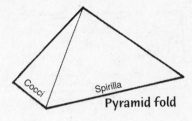

Pyramid fold

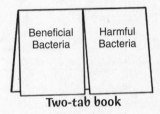

Two-tab book

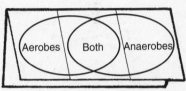

Three-tab Venn diagram

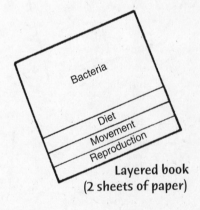

Layered book
(2 sheets of paper)

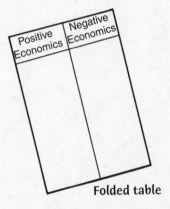

Folded table

Cells

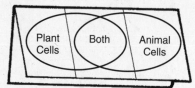

Three-tab Venn diagram

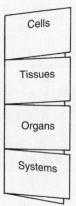

Four-tab book

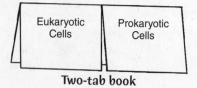

Four-door book

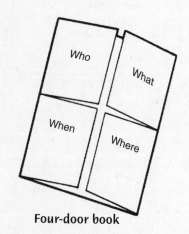

Two-tab book

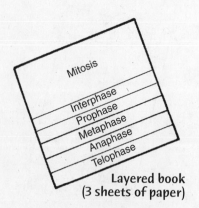

**Layered book
(3 sheets of paper)**

Skill	Activity Suggestion	Foldable Parts
compare and contrast	tissue and organs	2
	eukaryotic and prokaryotic cells	2
	plant and animal cells and tissues	2
	mitosis and meiosis	2
define	a cell as a basic unit of life or the basic building block of life	1
describe	cells, including living systems, regulated processes, and ability to reproduce	any number
	osmosis as it relates to cells	1
diagram	structure and purpose of the nucleus	2
	meiosis	any number
explain	the cell theory	1
	structure and purpose of a cell membrane	2
illustrate	the life cycle of a cell	any number
justify	cells being compared to building blocks	1
make a table	of the number of chromosome pairs in different organisms	any number
question	create a "know?-like to know?-learned?" about cells	3
research	largest and smallest cells	2
	cell walls in plants, fungi, and most bacteria	3
	endoplasmic reticulum and ribosomes	2
	the "who, what, when, where" of Robert Hooke	4
sequence	mitosis phases, including prophase, metaphase, anaphase, and telophase	4
summarize	how cell division differs in prokaryotic and eukaryotic cells	2

Ecosystems and Biomes

Skill	Activity Suggestion	Foldable Parts
	Desert	
compare and contrast	the world's deserts	2
	types of deserts by temperature	2
	soils rich in humus and desert soils	2
define	what conditions determine a desert	1
describe	a desert	1
diagram	ways in which desert plants store water, including swollen stems, leaves, and deep root systems	3
	the major deserts of each continent on a map	7
explain	why deserts are called "lands of extremes"	1
	polar deserts	1
	desert weathering, including water and wind	1
graph	examples of night and day air temperature variations in a desert	any number
	the percentage of the world's land that is desert	2
list	ways in which desert plants reduce water loss, including reducing the size of leaves or spines, waxy coating on leaves or stems, and closeable leaves	any number
locate	the world's subtropical geographic belts of deserts on a globe	1
make a table	on desert insects, arachnids, fish, amphibians, reptiles, birds, and mammals	any number
	of information on weather conditions in several deserts, including precipitation, windstorms, evaporation rate, and humidity level	any number
make a Venn diagram	labeled *semiarid desert, arid desert,* and *hyperarid desert*	3
question	create a "know?-like to know?-learned?" about deserts	3
research	different types of deserts, including sand dunes, rock, pebbled ground, and frozen	any number
	four common desert plants, possibly including cacti, yucca, mesquite, sagebrush, creosote bush, or annuals	4
	four desert animals, possibly including lizards, spiders, scorpions, snakes, or small mammals	4
	how desert animals have adapted to little water and high daytime heat, possibly including kangaroo rat, camels, reptiles, or fox	1
	past and present peoples of the desert	2
show cause and effect	of plant adaptations, including how plants have adapted to water storage	2
	of annual rainfall and life species in a desert	2
	of more plant biomass under soil than above	2

World Deserts
North America
South America
Europe
Asia
Australia
Antarctica
Africa

**Layered book
(4 sheets of paper)**

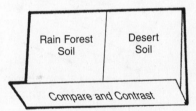

Folded table

Two-tab matchbook

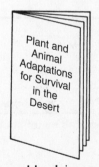

Bound-book journal

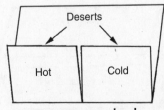

Concept-map book

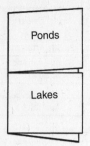

Ponds

Lakes

Two-tab book

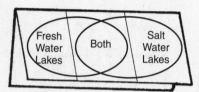

Fresh Water Lakes | Both | Salt Water Lakes

Three-tab Venn diagram

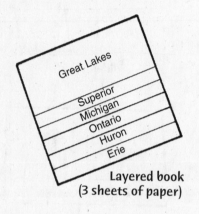

Great Lakes

Superior
Michigan
Ontario
Huron
Erie

**Layered book
(3 sheets of paper)**

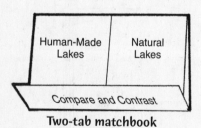

Human-Made Lakes | Natural Lakes

Compare and Contrast

Two-tab matchbook

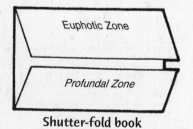

Euphotic Zone

Profundal Zone

Shutter-fold book

Freshwater: Lake and Pond

Skill	Activity Suggestion	Foldable Parts
compare and contrast	ponds and lakes	2
	freshwater lakes and salt lakes	2
	human-made and natural lakes	2
describe	the features of most lakes, including little water flow, mostly freshwater, constantly filling with sediment to become dry land, etc.	any number
diagram	lake layers, including hypolimnion, thermocline, and epilimnion	3
	the continents with the most and the fewest lakes on a map	2
	lake life zones, including euphotic zone and profundal zone	2
explain	how scientists know where ancient lakes were located	1
illustrate	the seasonal changes in a lake	4
list	ways in which lakes influence people's lives	any number
outline	how lakes can affect area weather, possibly including lake-effect snow, wind chill, area temperatures to lake water retaining heat	any number
prove	the statement "Lakes are short lived and are always shrinking."	1
question	create a "know?-like to know?-learned?" about lakes	3
research	salt and soda lakes, possibly including Caspian Sea, Utah's Great Salt Lake, the Dead Sea	any number
	three of the world's largest lakes	3
	lake and pond animals, possibly including fish, water birds, insects, snails, worms, zooplankton	any number
	diapause as it relates to lake and pond animals	1
	lake and pond plants, including phytoplankton and macrophytes	any number
	lake and pond insects, possibly including water beetles, mosquitoes, spiders, or dragonflies	any number
	Siberia's Lake Baikal	1
	the Great Lakes of North America, including Superior, Michigan, Ontario, Huron, and Erie	5
	the lakes of the Great Rift Valley, including Lake Tanganyika, Lake Albert, Lake Nyasa	3
	the "what, where, when, why" of Lake Texcoco lake bed	4
show cause and effect	of seiches and compare them to water being sloshed in a bucket	3
	of glacier movement and lake formation in the northern hemisphere	2

Freshwater: Rivers and Streams

Skill	Activity Suggestion	Foldable Parts
compare and contrast	a river and a stream	2
	flowing waters with nonflowing waters	2
	estuaries and rivers	2
examine	the relationship between rivers and industry in the past and present	2
explain	the Continental Divide as it relates to the flow of rivers	1
illustrate	the basic shapes of rivers, including straight streams, meandering streams, and braided streams	3
list	things that all rivers have in common, including one-way flow, fresh water, movement from higher to lower areas, more water at their mouth than their beginning, erosion, and shaping the land around them	any number
	pros and cons of dam construction	2
	advantages and disadvantages of seasonal flooding	2
	early civilizations named after the rivers on which they depended	any number
	the pros and cons of rivers used as recreation	2
make a timeline	of river transportation in the past, present, and predictions for the future	3
question	create a "know?-like to know?-learned?" about rivers and streams	3
research	three of the world's largest rivers, possibly including Amazon, Nile, Mississippi, Ganges, or Yangtze	3
	types of rivers, including permanent streams, intermittent streams, and interrupted streams	3
	animals living in moving water, possibly including greater number of species than in non-flowing; insects that have hooks, suckers, and adaptations to stay in place; animals that have eggs that are attached to plants or other bodies to stay in place	any number
	a river and its watershed or drainage basin	1
	several rivers of North America, possibly including Colorado, Snake, Rio Grande, Platte, Hudson, Swannee, Mississippi	any number
	aquifers	any number
show cause and effect	of fast-moving water versus slow-moving water	2
	of flash flooding	2
	of river pollution	2

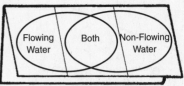

Three-tab Venn diagram

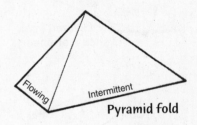

Pyramid fold

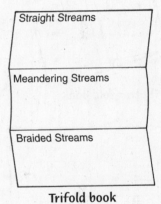

Trifold book

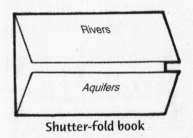

Shutter-fold book

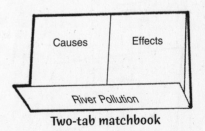

Two-tab matchbook

Grassland

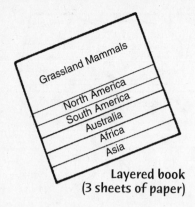

Grassland Mammals
North America
South America
Australia
Africa
Asia

Layered book
(3 sheets of paper)

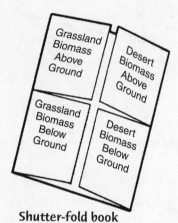

Grassland Biomass Above Ground | Desert Biomass Above Ground
Grassland Biomass Below Ground | Desert Biomass Below Ground

Shutter-fold book

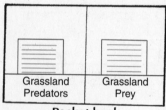

Grassland Predators | Grassland Prey

Pocket book

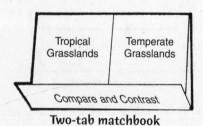

Tropical Grasslands | Temperate Grasslands

Compare and Contrast

Two-tab matchbook

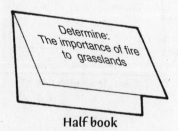

Determine:
The importance of fire to grasslands

Half book

Skill	Activity Suggestion	Foldable Parts
chart	worldwide names for grasslands, including veld in South Africa, steppe in Eurasia, rangeland in Australia, pampa in South American, and prairie in North America	5
compare and contrast	plant biomass of a grassland and a desert	2
	predators and their prey in different grasslands of the world	2
	grassland precipitation to that of another biome	2
determine	characteristics that grasslands have in common, including grasses, winds, dry climate, and few trees	any number
	the importance of fire to a grassland	1
diagram	the world's grasslands on a map	6
make a table	of information on grassland plants, possibly including grasses, forbs, wildflower species, cacti, shrubs, or trees	any number
outline	dangers to grasslands, possibly including overgrazing, farming, development, global climate change, introduction of exotic species, extracting mineral deposits, depositing toxic waste, or dumps in these areas	any number
predict	the effect of bringing in non-native species to a grassland	1
prove	the statement "Grasslands cover one fourth of Earth's land."	1
question	create a "know?-like to know?-learned?" about grasslands	3
research	grassland mammals by continent, possibly including pronghorn deer, bison, kangaroos, llamas, zebras, giraffes, or antelope	any number
	four burrowing grassland animals, possibly including prairie dogs, gophers, ground squirrels, burrowing owls, or wombats	4
	four different kinds of grass common to your area	4
	grassland insects, possibly including grasshoppers, locust, stinkbugs, ladybugs, scarab beetles, dragonflies, cicadas, or crickets	any number
	different kinds of grasslands, including tropical and temperate	2
	how different animals graze	any number
show cause and effect	of the Dust Bowl in the 1930s	2

Rain Forest

Skill	Activity Suggestion	Foldable Parts
chart	fish, amphibians, reptiles, birds, and mammals common to a specific rain forest	5
compare and contrast	between a rain forest and a deciduous forest biome	2
	seasonal changes in a rain forest to those in a deciduous forest	2
	the inner and outer regions of a rain forest	2
debate	mining in rain forests	2
	logging in rain forests	2
	clearing rain forests for cattle ranches	2
describe	a rain forest, including rainfall amount, temperature, vegetation, and humidity	4
diagram	the depth of light penetration in a typical rain forest	2
	the world's rain forests and note proximity to the equator on a map	any number
explain	predator/prey relationships of a selected rain forest	any number
	why there are few large mammals native to the rain forest, a few examples are okapi, mountain gorilla, orangutan, and sloth	1
graph	the percentage of plant and animal species on Earth that live in tropical rain forest ecosystems	2
	the percentage of light reaching different rain forest levels	any number
	the percentage of the South American continent that the Amazon rain forest covers (40%)	2
	statistics pertaining to rain forests past and present	2
hypothesize	as to why some of the world's largest and smallest plants and animals are found in rain forests	1
illustrate	layers of a rain forest, including emergent layer, canopy, understory, shrub layer, herb layer	5
	rain forest trees with buttresses and stilts	any number
	ways in which plants get rid of excess water	any number
justify	the movements to save the rain forests	any number
list	the advantages of being able to fly or glide in a rain forest, possibly focusing on squirrels, colugos, opossums, lizards, or snakes	any number
prove	the statement "The rain forest has the greatest amount of biomass of any biome."	1
question	create a "know?-like to know?-learned?" about rain forests	3
research	rain forest plants of South America, Africa, and Asia	3
	rain forest animals of South America, Africa, and Asia	3
	common epiphytes, including orchids, air plants, and bromeliads	any number
show cause and effect	of large amounts of precipitation	2
summarize	the importance of rain forest insects	1

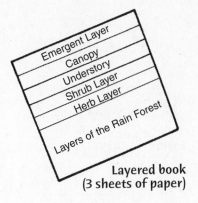

Layered book
(3 sheets of paper)

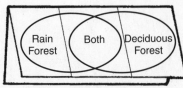

Three-tab Venn diagram

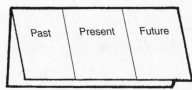

Three-tab book

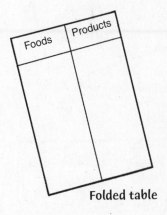

Folded table

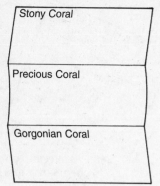

Trifold book

Stony Coral

Precious Coral

Gorgonian Coral

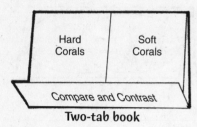

Two-tab book

Hard Corals	Soft Corals

Compare and Contrast

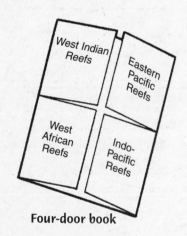

Four-door book

West Indian Reefs

Eastern Pacific Reefs

West African Reefs

Indo-Pacific Reefs

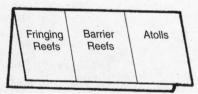

Three-tab book

Fringing Reefs	Barrier Reefs	Atolls

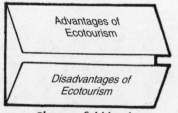

Shutter-fold book

Advantages of Ecotourism

Disadvantages of Ecotourism

Salt Water: Coral Reef

Skill	Activity Suggestion	Foldable Parts
chart	conditions needed for coral growth	any number
compare and contrast	types of coral, including stony coral, precious coral, and gorgonian coral	3
	colonizing coral with other colonizing animals	2
	the main kinds of corals, including reef building and non-reef building	2
	coral reefs and tropical rain forests	2
	types of coral reefs, including fringing reefs, barrier reefs, and atolls	3
diagram	the main geographic locations of coral reefs, including the Indo-Pacific region, West Indian region, Eastern Pacific region, and West African region on a map	4
	the zones of a coral reef, including lagoon, reef flat, reef crest, and fore-reef	4
explain	how coral animals form limestone structures	1
	the relationship between coral and the algae living inside them	2
hypothesize	how coral reefs are affected by global warming	1
illustrate	how ocean atolls originate from coral reefs	1
list	different kinds of stony coral	any number
make a table	imparting information on the general physical needs of coral reefs and data on specific reefs, including water temperature of at least 75 degrees Fahrenheit, grown near surface in clear waters, and grow mainly in the tropics	any number
prove	the statement "The Indo-Pacific reefs have the most variety of animal species."	1
	the statement "Coral reefs are both durable and sensitive at the same time."	2
question	create a "know?-like to know?-learned?" about coral	3
research	coral and explain how coral reefs are made	2
	animals that live on or near corals, possibly including sponges, lobsters, worms, fish, shrimp, or sea anemones	any number
	the four geographic coral reef locations, including the Indo-Pacific region, West Indian region, Eastern Pacific region, and West African region	4
	coral reef algae	any number
	the world's longest coral reefs, including the Great Barrier Reef and Belize Coral Reef	any number
	coral reef destruction since the 1960s by crown-of-thorns fish	1

Salt Water: Ocean

Skill	Activity Suggestion	Foldable Parts
chart	ocean predators and ocean prey	2
compare and contrast	ocean predators to land predators	2
	ocean prey to land prey	2
	ocean vertebrates and invertebrates	2
	types of plankton, including zooplankton and phytoplankton	any number
	ocean plants to land plants	2
	ocean animals to land animals	2
	ocean invertebrates to land invertebrates	2
diagram	levels of ocean life, including surface dwellers, free-swimmers, and bottom dwellers	any number
	an ocean food web	any number
	marine migratory routes on a map and explain them	2
explain	how marine organisms are part of the world food web	1
graph	ocean life (90% plankton, 10% other)	any number
hypothesize	about the effects of commercial collection of krill	any number
illustrate	surface dwellers, including plankton, jellyfish, by-the-wind sailors, Portuguese man-of-war	any number
	free-swimmers, called nekton, possibly including bony fish, cartilaginous fish, squid, marine reptiles, or marine mammals	any number
	photic zone to no light zone	2
	and list examples of zooplankton	any number
	and list examples of phytoplankton	any number
make a chart	on the life styles of several specific ocean animals, possibly including how they obtain oxygen, food and water, regulate temperature, or move	any number
make a diorama	of a habitat within the ocean, possibly including coral reef, ocean floor, kelp forest, or sunken ship	any number
	of levels of life in the ocean	any number
make a model	of an ocean animal	any number
question	create a "know?-like to know?-learned?" about oceans	3
research	producers, consumers, and decomposers as they relate to oceans	3
	marine fish, reptiles, birds, and mammals	4
	life adapted to ocean depths	1
	life adapted to tidal zones	1
	different kinds of seaweed	any number
	cause and effect of ocean pollution on ocean life	2
	endangered ocean species	any number
	the "what, where, when, how/why" of the Exxon Valdez oil spill in 1989 or the Sargasso Sea	4

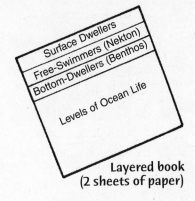

**Layered book
(2 sheets of paper)**

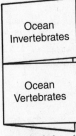

**Two-tab book
(vertical)**

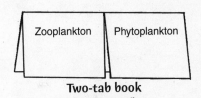

**Two-tab book
(horizontal)**

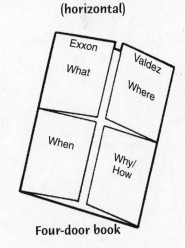

Four-door book

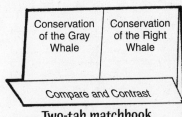

Two-tab matchbook

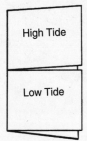

High Tide

Low Tide

Two-tab book

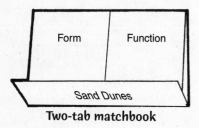

| Animals that anchor to rocks | Animals that hide in crevices | Animals with suction-cup feet | Animals that burrow |

Four-tab book

Upper Intertidal

Middle Intertidal

Pyramid fold

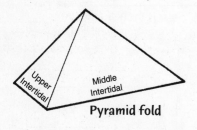

Form | Function

Sand Dunes

Two-tab matchbook

Sand (Located)	Formation	Size	Color

Folded table

Salt Water: Seashore

Skill	Activity Suggestion	Foldable Parts
chart	ways in which seashores are affected by storms	any number
compare and contrast	life found on rocky and sandy beaches	2
diagram	three seashore life zones, including upper intertidal, middle intertidal, and lower intertidal	3
	divisions of a seashore, including supralittoral, littoral, and sublittoral	3
	the United States's national seashores, including Cape Cod, Fire Island, Assateague Island, Cape Hatteras, Capte Lookout, Cumberland Island, Canaveral, Gulf Islands, Padre Island, and Point Reyes on a map	any number
explain	the statement "Land and sea are constantly playing tug-of-war."	1
	the seashore as an ecotone	1
	how sand dunes are formed and factors that can destroy them	2
list	pros and cons of constructing buildings on beaches	2
	advantages and disadvantages of motorized vehicles on beaches	2
observe	sand, including formation, sizes, and colors	3
prove	the statement "The border between land and sea is constantly changing."	1
question	create a "know?-like to know?-learned?" about seashores	3
research	two main types of seashores, including rocky and sandy beach	2
	upper intertidal life, possibly including algae, lichens, limpets, and barnacles	any number
	middle intertidal life, possibly including sea weeds, barnacles, chitons, limpets, corals, sea stars, anemones, worms, mussels, and crabs	any number
	lower intertidal life, possibly including sea weeds, anemones, sea slugs, sea urchins, sea stars, sea cucumbers, sea spiders, brittle stars, clams, mussels, or limpets	any number
	shore animals during high and low tides	2
	regions of life by levels	any number
	animals that stick to rocks, including limpets, barnacles, and mussels	any number
	animals that hide in crevices, including snails and crabs	any number
	animals with tube feet, including sea stars and sea cucumbers	any number
	burrowing animals, including worms, sand dollars, crabs, and clams	any number
	common seashore plants, including sea weeds, phytoplankton, and algae that grow on rocks	any number
	shorebirds and identify them as predators of the seashore	2
	nesting grounds for birds and sea turtles	any number
show cause and effect	of a rise in Earth's average temperature by even a few degrees on the shoreline	2

Taiga

Skill	Activity Suggestion	Foldable Parts
chart	taiga predators and their prey	any number
compare and contrast	taiga in North America, Asia, and Europe	3
	average rainfall of taiga with another biome	2
develop	a taiga food chain	any number
explain	the statement "Bodies of people and animals, as well as pollen from plants, thousands of years old can be found preserved in peat moss bogs."	1
	the taiga's location relative to other biomes	1
prove	that the taiga is the largest land biome using a map	1
question	create a "know?-like to know?-learned?" about taiga	3
research	taiga species' diversity	any number
	taiga plants, including evergreen coniferous trees, some broad-leafed deciduous trees, and unusual plants like pitcher plants	3
	taiga animals, possibly including caribou, wolverines, beaver, fish, water birds, or insects	any number
	what part the taiga plays in the migration and nesting of tropical birds	2
	peat moss bogs	1
	other names for this region, including boreal forest and northern coniferous forest	any number
	average temperature ranges	2

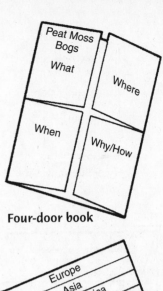

Four-door book

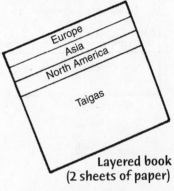

**Layered book
(2 sheets of paper)**

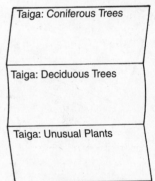

Trifold book

Half book

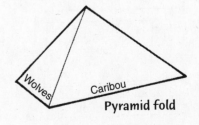

Pyramid fold

Arctic
Tundra

Alpine
Tundra

Two-tab book

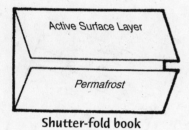

Active Surface Layer

Permafrost

Shutter-fold book

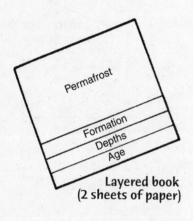

Permafrost

Formation
Depths
Age

**Layered book
(2 sheets of paper)**

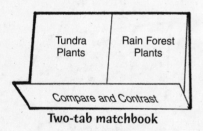

Tundra
Plants

Rain Forest
Plants

Compare and Contrast

Two-tab matchbook

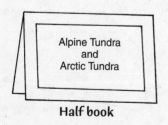

Alpine Tundra
and
Arctic Tundra

Half book

Tundra

Skill	Activity Suggestion	Foldable Parts
analyze	threats to the tundra, including pollution, ozone depletion, development, mining, overhunting, and fishing	any number
compare and contrast	different types of tundra, including arctic and alpine	2
	tundra and grassland plants and animals	2
	species diversity of the tundra to other biomes	2
	tundra and a desert	2
debate	mining or drilling for oil in tundra regions	2
	the statement "Even footsteps can cause damage in a tundra biome."	2
diagram	the Arctic tundra regions, including Alaska, Canada, Greenland, Iceland, Russia, and Scandinavia on a map	6
	the Alpine tundra regions on a map	any number
	tundra soil layers, including active surface soil and permafrost	2
graph	the percentage of Earth's land that is tundra	2
	the rate at which tundra plants grow compared to plants in another biome	2
list	ways in which animals deal with intense cold	any number
question	create a "know?-like to know?-learned?" about tundra	3
research	tundra weather, including temperatures, snow, rain, humidity, and wind	5
	archaeological discoveries in permafrost	any number
	permafrost, including formation, depth, and age	3
	tundra plants, possibly including mosses, lichens, sedges, shrubs, buttercups, poppies, or willows	any number
	lichens, including algae and fungi	2
	tundra mammals, possibly including arctic tern, caribou, musk oxen, lemmings, bears, hares, or weasels	any number
	the forces that shape the tundra, including freezing and thawing	any number
	peoples of the tundra past and present	2

Fungi

Skill	Activity Suggestion	Foldable Parts
classify	fungi by the structures in which they produce spores, including zygote fungi, sac fungi, club fungi, and imperfect fungi	4
compare and contrast	past and present classification of fungi	2
describe	how yeast makes bread dough rise	any number
	mold growing on bread or fruit	1
develop	a mushroom identification chart	any number
diagram	parts of fungi, including hyphae, mycelium, fruiting body, and spores	any number
	a life line of a fungus from spore to spore-producing organisms	any number
discuss	fungi as nature's recycler or decompose	1
explain	how litmus paper is made from a lichen called canary weed	1
	the important role fungi play in Earth's biosphere	1
make a timeline	illustrating the development of antibiotics, including penicillin from *Penicillium* mold	any number
make a Venn diagram	labeled *fungus, alga,* and *lichen formed by both*	3
observe	mildew	1
outline	fungi's relationship with humankind, possibly including medicines, food, and disease	any number
question	create a "know?-like to know?-learned?" about fungi	3
research	four types of fungi, possibly including yeast, molds, mushrooms, lichen, truffles, puffballs, or bucket fungi	4
	different ways in which fungi obtain food, including saprophytes, symbionts, and parasites	3
	positive and negative effects of fungi	2
	different types of lichen and explain how they are part of a food chain	2
	the part lichens play in eroding sedimentary rock	1
	why lichens are called pioneer species	1
	fungi reproduction	1
	how yeast can produce sexually and asexually by budding	2
	the commercial importance of mushrooms and how they are formed	2
	the use of truffles in French cooking, past and present	2
show cause and effect	of fungi in cheese and wine production	2
summarize	the symbiotic relationship between fungi and algae that form lichen, including alga or cyanobacterium and a fungus	2
write	an essay on the dangers of gathering and consuming wild mushrooms	1

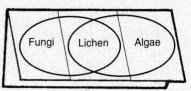

Three-tab Venn diagram

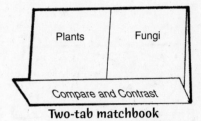

Two-tab matchbook

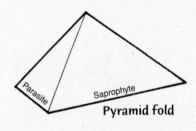

Pyramid fold

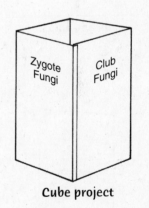

Cube project

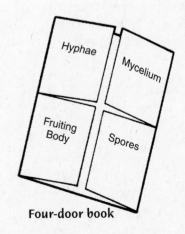

Four-door book

Heredity

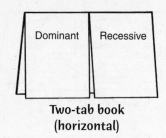

Two-tab book
(horizontal)

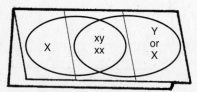

Three-tab Venn diagram

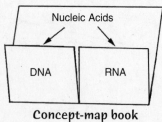

Concept-map book

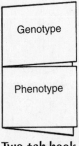

Two-tab book
(vertical)

Skill	Activity Suggestion	Foldable Parts
compare and contrast	body cells and sex cells	2
	genes to blueprints used by builders	2
	characteristics resulting from heredity and environment	2
	natural selection, evolution, and selective breeding	3
define	alleles	1
	traits and list examples of traits	2
describe	form and function of chromosomes	2
	two types of nucleic acids, including DNA and RNA	2
determine	cause and effect of dominant and recessive genes	2
discuss	what makes each kind of living thing genetically unique	1
explain	how genes carry traits from one generation to another	1
	chromosomes of offspring in asexual and sexual reproduction	2
	form and function of chromosomes	2
	the genome of a species	1
list	examples of hereditary diseases	any number
make a concept map	for population as it relates to heredity	any number
make a table	of organisms and how many chromosomes they have	any number
make a timeline	on the study of heredity or genetics	any number
make a Venn diagram	labeled *eggs = X, sperm = Y,* and *baby = XX* or *YY*	3
question	create a "know?-like to know?-learned?" about heredity	3
research	and make Punnett squares	any number
	X and Y chromosomes found in humans	2
	the composition of DNA, including phosphate, deoxyribose, adenine, guanine, thymine, and cytosine	6
	Mendel's Laws of Heredity	2
	how and why genetic mutations occur	2
	genetic recombinations, including crossing over and assortment of genes on different chromosomes	2
	the "who, what, when, where" of Chevalier de Lamarck or Gregor Mendel	4
write	about your traits	any number

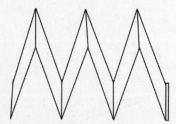

Timeline: History of
the Study of Genetics

Human Body

Skill	Activity Suggestion	Foldable Parts
compare and contrast	the human body to a machine	2
	the amount of water in a human body to the amount of water in other living organisms	2
	human brain to brains of other animals, possibly including size, intelligence, and memory	2
define	tissues	1
	organs	1
describe	the function of every cell in the body, including taking in food, ridding itself of waste, and growing	3
explain	why humans are vertebrates and mammals	2
graph	how water comprises about 65 percent of the human body	2
list	and describe the five senses of the human body, including taste, smell, sight, hearing, and touch	5
question	create a "know?-like to know?-learned?" about the human body	3
research	what the human body needs to take in, including food and oxygen	2
	the four most common chemical elements in the human body, including carbon, hydrogen, nitrogen, oxygen	4
	the significance of the element carbon to living organisms	1
	other elements important for a healthy body, including calcium, iron, phosphorus, potassium and sodium	5
	water as it relates to the most common molecule in the human body	1
	macromolecules in the human body, including carbohydrates, lipids, proteins, and nucleic acids	4
	four different types of tissues, including connective, epithelial, muscle, and nervous	4
	systems of the human body	any number

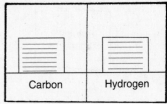

Pocket book

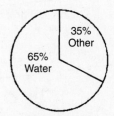

Circle graph

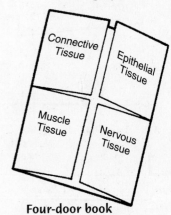

Four-door book

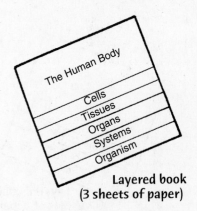

Layered book
(3 sheets of paper)

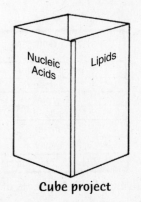

Cube project

Life: General

Two-tab book

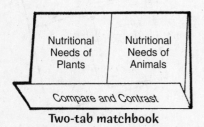

Half book

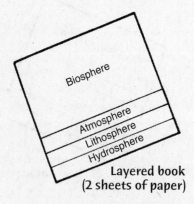

Two-tab matchbook

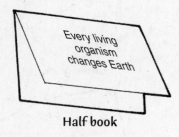

**Layered book
(2 sheets of paper)**

Layered book (4 sheets of paper)

Skill	Activity Suggestion	Foldable Parts
chart	the six kingdoms, including Archaebacteria, Eubacteria, Protista, Fungi, Plantae, Animalia	6
compare and contrast	living organisms that produce their own food and those that depend upon other organisms for food	2
	terrestrial and marine organisms	2
	organic and inorganic matter	2
	the study of prehistoric life to current life	2
	living organisms and viruses	2
	plant and animal cells	2
	a food chain, a food pyramid, and a food web	3
define	biology as the study of all living things	1
describe	the importance of water to past, present, and future life	3
diagram	a cross-section of Earth's biosphere, including part of Earth above and below ground in which life exists	2
	several food chains	any number
discuss	the statement "Every living organism changes Earth."	1
explain	the statement "Living organisms are matter and energy that use the matter and energy around them to survive."	1
	the importance of the Sun to past, present, and future life	3
hypothesize	what planet Earth would be like if life did not nor had never existed	1
list	pros and cons of a one-celled life and a many-celled life	2
outline	six characteristics all living organisms have in common	6
question	create a "know?-like to know?-learned?" about life	3
research	what things living organisms need to survive and reproduce, including food, water, gases, appropriate habitat, mate of same species	any number
	one-celled life, including archaebacteria, eubacteria, and protists	3
	many-celled life, including fungi, plants, and animals	3
	saprophytes, including fungi and bacteria	2
	the roles of producers, consumers, and decomposers	3
	the "who, what, when, where" of important biologists of past and present	4
show cause and effect	of living organisms that change Earth slightly and those that change it drastically	2

Nutrition

Skill	Activity Suggestion	Foldable Parts
chart	information pertaining to each of the five food groups	5
compare and contrast	nutritional needs of plants and animals	2
	vegetable protein and meat protein	2
	typical daily food intake, past and present	2
	food that is and is not grown organically	2
	natural and artificial foods	2
debate	the validity of a current diet fad	2
determine	what would happen if a person did not eat a nutritious diet	1
evaluate	your own diet and the diet of a friend	2
explain	the purpose of food additives	1
	why nitrates are added to foods	1
justify	the statement "A good diet is essential to growth and well being."	1
	government requirements regarding food labeling	1
list	pros and cons of vegetarianism	2
make a table	of nutritional information on foods you like to eat	any number
observe	if the restaurants you visit provide nutritional food for special diets	1
plan	a balanced diet on a low budget	any number
question	create a "know?-like to know?-learned?" about nutrition	3
research	the effects of malnutrition	any number
	the causes and effects of obesity	2
	effects of diet on hyperactivity	2
	common food allergies	any number
	scurvy and its impact on early exploration	2
show cause and effect	of poverty and nutrition	2

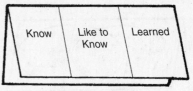

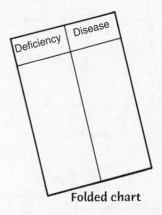

Three-tab book

Folded chart

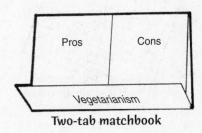

Bound-book journal

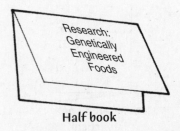

Two-tab matchbook

Half book

Plants

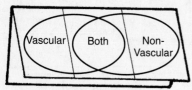

Three-tab Venn diagram

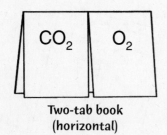

**Two-tab book
(horizontal)**

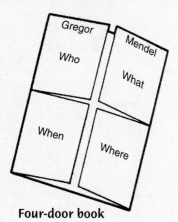

Four-door book

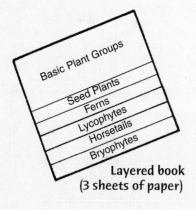

**Layered book
(3 sheets of paper)**

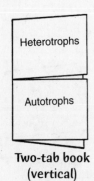

**Two-tab book
(vertical)**

Skill	Activity Suggestion	Foldable Parts
chart	nonvascular plants, including liverworts, hornworts, and mosses	any number
	vascular plants, including club mosses, horsetails, ferns, and seed plants	any number
compare and contrast	nonvascular and vascular plants	2
	the basic groups of plants, including seed plants, ferns, lycophytes, horsetails, and bryophytes	5
	land and water plants	2
	positive and negative tropisms	2
	day-flowering plants and night-flowering plants	2
describe	and list the scientific classification of plants into divisions	10
diagram	plant respiration	any number
	vascular tissue, including xylem and phloem	2
	the parts of a flowering plant	any number
explain	the importance of cellulose for support and retention of water	1
	the work of different kinds of specialized botanists	any number
	the importance of cholorplasts and chlorophyll	2
graph	some of the world's largest plants, living or extinct	2
	some of the world's smallest plants, living or extinct	2
	average life span of selected plants	any number
illustrate	a plant cell	any number
list	advantages and disadvantages of plants living on land	2
make a Venn diagram	labeled *animal cell, plant cell,* and *both*	3
	labeled *seed plants, seedless plants,* and *both*	3
observe	a plant with a cuticle	1
	perennial and annual plants	2
outline	the movement of water through a plant	any number
question	create a "know?-like to know?-learned?" about plants	3
research	fossil evidence of plants	1
	characteristics of plants	4
	how plants get food, including autotrophs and heterotrophs	2
	plants with little or no chlorophyll	any number
	carnivorous insect-eating plants	any number
	the "who, what, when, where" of any of the following people: Carolus Linnaeus, Gregor Mendel, or Barbara McClintock	4
show cause and effect	of transpiration	2
summarize	photosynthesis	any number
	the importance of plants in our daily lives	any number

Division Bryophyta: Liverworts and Mosses

Skill	Activity Suggestion	Foldable Parts
compare and contrast	plants with and without vascular tissue	2
	bryophyte forms, including gametophyte and sporophyte	2
describe	how bryophytes are used as nesting materials by hummingbirds	1
explain	why bryophytes are often referred to as pioneer species	1
	bryophytes' need for moisture to reproduce	1
graph	average sizes of several bryophytes	any number
	the numbers of species of liverworts (9,000) and mosses (14,000)	2
identify	and define bryophytes	2
make a Venn diagram	labeled *rhizoids*, *roots*, and *both*	3
question	create a "know?-like to know?-learned?" about bryophytes	3
research	Class Hepaticae (liverworts)	any number
	Class Anthocerotae (hornworts)	any number
	Class Muscopsida (true mosses)	any number
	peat moss used as a fuel	1
	the environmental importance of mosses	any number
	how sphagnum moss can help prevent the growth of certain disease-causing bacteria	1
sequence	the steps in the formation of peat moss	any number

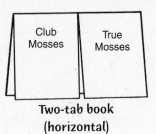

Two-tab book (horizontal)

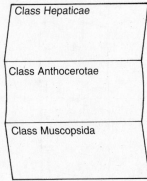

Trifold book

Division Psilophyta: Wisk Ferns

Skill	Activity Suggestion	Foldable Parts
diagram	the reproductive cycle	any number
	the tropical and subtropical habitats of whisk ferns on a map	2
list	three characteristics of wisk ferns	3
question	create a "know?-like to know?-learned?" about psilophytes	3
research	*Psilotum nudum* and *Phynia gwynnevaughanii*	2

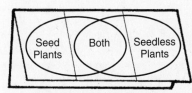

Three-tab Venn diagram

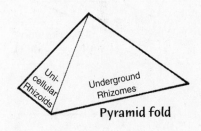

Pyramid fold

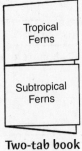

Two-tab book (vertical)

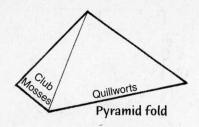
Pyramid fold

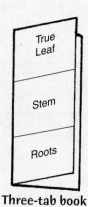
Three-tab book

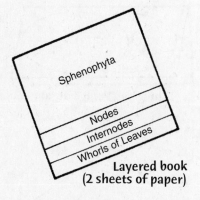
**Layered book
(2 sheets of paper)**

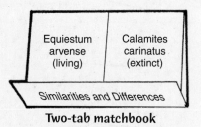
Two-tab matchbook

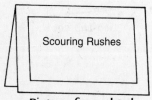
Picture-frame book

Division Lycophyta: Club Mosses

Skill	Activity Suggestion	Foldable Parts
compare and contrast	treelike club moss fossils to living plants	2
diagram	a club moss and show it has true leaf, stem, and root systems	3
explain	why club mosses are not true mosses	1
	how club mosses helped form modern coal beds	1
question	create a "know?-like to know?-learned?" about lycophytes	3
research	lycophytes, including club mosses, quillworts, and selaginellas	3
	why these plants are threatened	1

Division Sphenophyta: Horsetails

Skill	Activity Suggestion	Foldable Parts
compare and contrast	treelike fossil horsetails and living plants	2
	Equisetum avense and *Calamites carinatus*	2
describe	physical characteristics of sphenophytes, including jointed stems that form nodes, internodes, and whorls of leaves	3
hypothesize	as to why these plants were called "scouring rushes" by American colonists	1
question	create a "know?-like to know?-learned?" about horsetails	3
research	different kinds of horsetails including scouring rush	any number
	the one living genus of horsetail	1

Division Pterophyta: Ferns

Skill	Activity Suggestion	Foldable Parts
collect	fern fronds	any number
diagram	parts of a fern, including stem, roots, and leaves	3
graph	fern sizes	any number
	the percentage of fern species found in the tropics	2
hypothesize	how fiddleheads got their name	1
identify	edible ferns and develop a recipe for serving them	2
illustrate	fronds of different sizes and shapes	any number
list	characteristics of ferns	any number
	pros and cons of spore reproduction	2
make a timeline	of ferns known through fossil records to present	any number
observe	two types of fern leaves, fertile and sterile	2
outline	the formation of coal and explain the economic impact prehistoric plants like ferns still have on the world economy	2
question	create a "know?-like to know?-learned?" about ferns	3
research	stages of growth and reproduction, including sexual and asexual	2
	tree-sized ferns found in Hawaii and explain why ferns can grow taller than mosses	2
	North American ferns, possibly including bracken, royal fern, or Western sword fern	any number
	ferns grown commercially	any number
	Azolla and its mutualistic relationship with a cyanobacterium called *Anabaena azollae*	1
write	a manual explaining how to raise and care for fern plants	any number

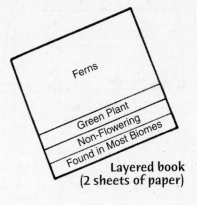

**Layered book
(2 sheets of paper)**

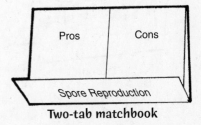

Two-tab matchbook

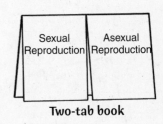

Circle graph

Two-tab book

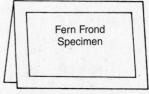

Picture-frame book

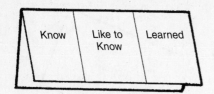

Three-tab book
(horizontal)

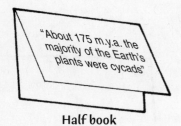

"About 175 m.y.a. the majority of the Earth's plants were cycads"

Half book

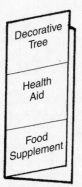

Three-tab book
(vertical)

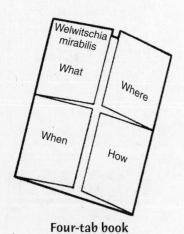

Four-tab book

Division Cyadophyta: Cycads

Skill	Activity Suggestion	Foldable Parts
describe	how cycads reproduce	any number
hypothesize	why once-common cycads are rare today	1
illustrate	the physical characteristics of cycads	any number
map	locations of modern cycads, including tropics and subtropics	2
question	create a "know?-like to know?-learned?" about cycads	3
research	when the majority of Earth's plants were cycads	1
	the cone of a cycad	1

Division Ginkgophyta: Ginkgoes

Skill	Activity Suggestion	Foldable Parts
hypothesize	why ginkgoes are no longer found in the wild	1
question	create a "know?-like to know?-learned?" about ginkgoes	3
research	the one species of ginkgo living today	1
	how Chinese and Japanese gardeners have preserved this plant	1
	ginkgoes being grown in cities because they can tolerate air pollution	1
	the use of ginkgo as a health aid and food supplement	1

Division Gnetophyta: Gnetophytes

Skill	Activity Suggestion	Foldable Parts
diagram	the Namib Desert in Africa on a map	1
question	create a "know?-like to know?-learned?" about gnetophytes	3
research	the three genera of gnetophytes, including Ephedra, Gnetum, and Witschia	3
	the "what, where, when, how" of *Welwitschia mirabilis* found in the Namib desert	4

Division Coniferophyta: Conifers

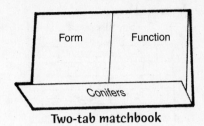

Form | Function

Conifers

Two-tab matchbook

Skill	Activity Suggestion	Foldable Parts
chart	information on several different species of conifers, including location, height, and cones	any number
collect	different conifer leaves	any number
compare and contrast	cypress trees to other conifers	2
debate	the pros and cons of using redwood and cypress for lumber	2
determine	why conifers can withstand extremely cold temperatures	1
	why conifers are called "softwood trees"	1
explain	the advantages of producing male and female cones on one tree	1
	why conifers are usually referred to as "evergreens"	1
graph	the heights of different conifers	any number
illustrate	and describe conifer leaves	2
list	important products from gymnosperms, including resins, seeds, lumber, and mulch	any number
question	create a "know?-like to know?-learned?" about conifers	3
research	bristlecone pines	1
	different types of redwood trees	any number
	construction advantages to using redwood	any number
	the "who, what, when, where" of Robert Brown	4
sequence	the discovery and commercial production of taxol as a treatment for certain kinds of cancer	any number

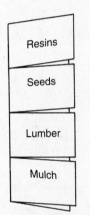

	Redwood	Pine	Cypress
Location			
Height			
Cones			

Folded table

Resins

Seeds

Lumber

Mulch

Four-tab book

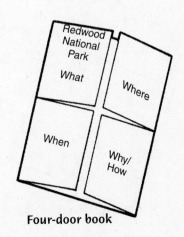

Redwood National Park

What

Where

When

Why/How

Four-door book

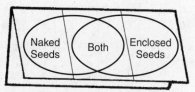

Seed Dispersal
Helicopters
Hitchhikers
Parachutes
Delectables
Floaters
Missiles
Vocabulary

**Layered book
(4 sheets of paper)**

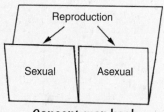

Three-tab Venn diagram

Reproduction → Sexual, Asexual

Concept-map book

Angiosperms
Gymnosperms

Two-tab book

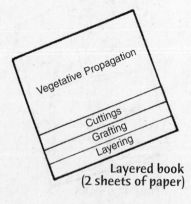

Vegetative Propagation
Cuttings
Grafting
Layering

**Layered book
(2 sheets of paper)**

Division Anthophyta: Angiosperms
(Seeds and Seed Plants)

Skill	Activity Suggestion	Foldable Parts
collect	different seeds and sketch or trace around them	any number
compare and contrast	types of seed plants, including flowering and nonflowering	2
	largest and smallest angiosperms	2
	seed development in angiosperms and gymnosperms	2
	self pollination and cross pollination	2
define	angiosperms	1
describe	different ways in which seeds disperse, including helicopters, hitchhikers, parachute, delectables, floaters, and missiles	any number
diagram	parts of a seedling, including hypocotyls, epicotyl, and plumule	3
	the parts of a seed	any number
	the arrangement of vascular bundles in monocots and dicots	2
	forests of the most common gymnosperms on a map	any number
explain	the cause and effect of seed dormancy	2
graph	seeds of different sizes	any number
	seed record setters	any number
illustrate	the pollination of a seed plant, including pollen moving from anther to pistil	any number
list	characteristics of seeds	3
	characteristics of gymnosperms	any number
	examples of gymnosperms, possibly including conifers, cycads, ginkgoes, and gnetophytes	any number
make a table	of the number of seeds that selected plants produce	any number
make a Venn diagram	labeled *naked seeds, enclosed seeds,* and *both*	3
	labeled *monocotyledons, dicotyledons,* and *both*	3
outline	the needs of seeds, including proper temperature, moisture, and oxygen to grow	3
	methods of vegetative propagation, including cuttings, grafting, and layering	3
prove	the statement "Seed plants compose the largest group of plants."	1
	the statement "There is no relationship between seed size and the size of a plant."	1
question	create a "know?-like to know?-learned?" about seed plants	3
research	and list examples of angiosperms	any number
	and list monocots, possibly including corn, bananas, or pineapples	any number
	and list dicots, possibly including peas, beans, squash, peanuts, or tomatoes	any number
	reproduction in plants	2
	pros and cons of self pollination and cross pollination	2
	cross-pollination helpers, including wind, insects, birds, and bats	4
	common and uncommon uses of seeds	2

Plant Parts: Leaves

Skill	Activity Suggestion	Foldable Parts
collect	leaves of different shapes	any number
	leaves of different sizes	any number
compare and contrast	simple and compound leaves	2
	leaves of plants in tropical and grassland biomes	2
	leaves and thorns	2
describe	the relationship between stomata and guard cells	2
design an experiment	to show transpiration as part of the water cycle	any number
diagram	the parts of a leaf, including blade, petiole, stipules, and veins	5
	the cross section of a leaf	any number
	the form and function of a rain forest leaf with a drip point	2
document	how many leaves you eat, possibly including lettuce, celery, cabbage, mint, basil, bay leaves, or turnip greens	any number
estimate	the leaf surface area of a plant	1
explain	how leaves produce food by a process called photosynthesis	any number
	the purpose of the cuticle on a leaf's surface	1
	cause and effect of a tree's leaves turning colors and then dropping	2
	and give examples of leaf adaptations to limit evaporation or transpiration, possibly including leaves opening and closing, waxy coating, reduction in size	any number
graph	variation in leaf size from smallest to largest	any number
list	advantages and disadvantages of leaves being the main plant part involved in photosynthesis	2
	advantages and disadvantages of seasonal leaf loss	2
make a chart	of plants with the three different arrangements of leaves	3
make a timeline	on the use of tobacco leaves	any number
observe	a green leaf by rubbing it on a piece of paper and describing what happens	2
	leaves as an important form of shade	1
	leaves as symbols, including the maple leaf of Canada and the fig leaf	any number
outline	the process of transpiration and explain its importance	2
predict	where the stomata of floating leaves will be found	1
prove	the statement "Some leaves provide a cooler shade than others."	1
question	create a "know?-like to know?-learned?" about leaves	3
research	leaf arrangements, including alternate or spiral, opposite, and whorled	3
	leaf shapes, including simple, compound, scalelike, needlelike, and spinelike	5
	the history of the poinsettia plant	1
	the history of salicylic acid which is used in aspirin	any number
	past and present use of tea leaves	2
	how some plants have sensitive leaves when touched	any number
	plants with poisonous leaves, including poison ivy and poison oak	any number
	the "who, what, where, when" of Stephen Hales	4

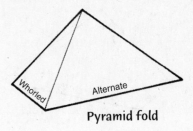

Pyramid fold

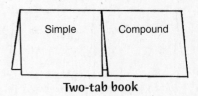

Two-tab book

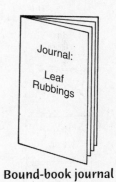

Bound-book journal

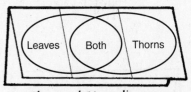

Three-tab Venn diagram

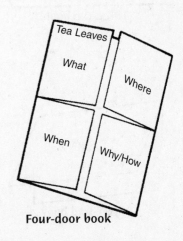

Four-door book

Plant Parts: Roots

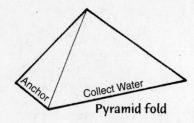
Pyramid fold

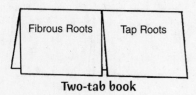
Two-tab book

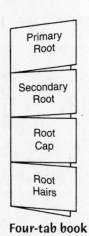
Four-tab book

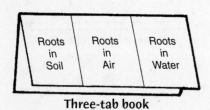
Three-tab book

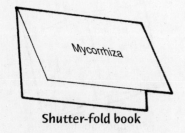
Shutter-fold book

Skill	Activity Suggestion	Foldable Parts
compare and contrast	primary roots and secondary roots	2
	fibrous and taproot systems	2
	roots found in soil, water, and air	3
	prop roots, aerial roots, and below-ground root systems	3
describe	the form and function of the primary root, secondary root, root cap, and root hairs	4
diagram	a fibrous root system like grass	1
	a taproot system like carrot	1
explain	how and why some roots act as a storage area for food	2
	how roots help prevent soil erosion	1
graph	lengths of some common roots	any number
illustrate	how plant roots provide maximum surface area exposure to soil to collect water and nutrients	1
list	examples of roots that store food, possibly including carrots, beets, turnips, yams, radishes, or sugar beets	any number
question	create a "know?-like to know?-learned?" about roots	3
research	cassava	1
	the use of roots as food or seasoning, possibly including licorice, horseradish, sassafras, or sugar beets	any number
	banyan trees and their root systems	1
	legumes as a natural fertilizer, possibly including peas, beans, clover, peanuts, or soybeans	any number
	mycorrhiza, which is a symbiotic relationship between vascular plant roots and fungi	1
	how and why chicory has been used as a coffee substitute	2
	cortisone	1
	whether the following wives tales are true or false: 1) a tree's roots extend to its leaf line and 2) a tree's tap root is as deep as the tree is tall	2
	the "what, where, when, how" of marshmallows	4
write	about the main purposes of roots, including anchor, collecting nutrients from soil, and collecting water	3

Plant Parts: Stems

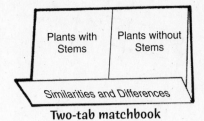

Two-tab matchbook

Skill	Activity Suggestion	Foldable Parts
compare and contrast	plants with and without stems	2
	trunks, limbs, stems, and twigs	4
	a tomato plant stem to a redwood tree trunk	2
	human use of stems to that of other animals	2
	bulbs and tubers	2
define	stems in terms of transport and support	2
describe	petrified forests	1
diagram	the cross section of a woody stem, including primary and secondary xylem, cambium, secondary phloem, phelloderm, cork cambium, and cork	8
	the stem of a cabbage	1
explain	woody and herbaceous aerial stems	2
	the purpose of the xylem and phloem	2
	the effect of cutting stems	1
graph	average circumference and length of common stems	any number
illustrate	aerial and subterranean stems	2
	form and function of herbaceous stems' primary tissue, including epidermis, phloem, xylem, and parenchyma	4
	how rhizomes grow	1
list	examples of plants with woody stems and herbaceous stems	2
	common and uncommon uses of stems, possibly including rubber, food production, timber industry, cork bark, or linen produced from plant stem fiber	any number
make a table	of information on common stems, including plant, stem circumference, and stem length	3
make a Venn diagram	labeled *woody stems*, *herbaceous stems*, and *both*	3
observe	specialized stems that enable plants to climb	any number
outline	maple syrup production	any number
question	create a "know?-like to know?-learned?" about stems	3
research	the main purpose of stems, including the production and support of buds, leaves, flowers, and fruit, as well as the transport of water and nutrients	2
	terminal and lateral buds	2
	and diagram a xylem cell	2
	stems that store water	1
	stems as a food source, possibly including cacti, asparagus, potatoes, or onions	any number
	the uses of bamboo, possibly including furniture, buildings, and musical instruments	any number
	the "what, where, when, why" of saguaro	4

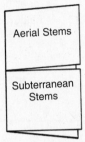

Two-tab book (vertical)

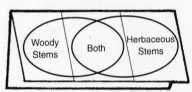

Three-tab Venn diagram

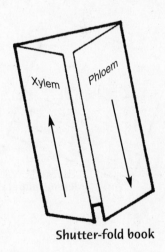

Shutter-fold book

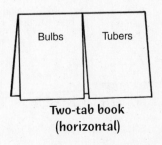

Two-tab book (horizontal)

Senses

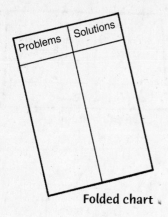

Folded chart

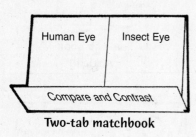

Two-tab matchbook

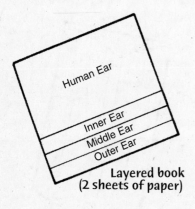

Layered book
(2 sheets of paper)

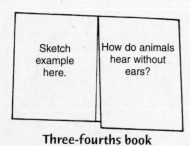

Three-fourths book

Sight: Eyes

Skill	Activity Suggestion	Foldable Parts
compare and contrast	the human eye to an insect eye	2
	near-sighted vision and far-sighted vision	2
	eyes of other animals to the human eye	2
	a human eyelid to a bird's eyelid	2
debate	the statement "Eye structure and function is similar in all animals."	2
define	color vision and color blindness	2
diagram	the human eye, including cornea, iris, pupil, lens, retina, and optic nerve	6
explain	the use of convex and concave lenses to correct vision	2
graph	sizes of different animal eyes	any number
identify	problems and solutions to vision requirements of animals living in total darkness	2
illustrate	the visible parts of the eye, including white and iris	2
list	animals with good nocturnal vision and diurnal vision	2
make a chart	of different animals, their eye positions, and eye size	any number
question	create a "know?-like to know?-learned?" about eyes	3
research	purposes of the dilator muscle and sphincter muscle	2

Hearing: Ears

Skill	Activity Suggestion	Foldable Parts
chart	animals with and without ears	2
describe	ear locations as they relate to sound detection	1
diagram	the human ear, including inner ear, middle ear, and outer ear	3
	the middle ear, including ear drum, chamber, auditory ossicles (3 bones), anvil, and stirrup	any number
	the inner ear, including vestibule, semicircular canals, and cochlea	3
	the human outer ear, including auricle and external auditory canal	2
	parts of the auricle, including cartilage, skin, earlobe, and fat	4
discuss	problems and solutions for animals without ears needed to hear	2
graph	sizes of animal ears	any number
list	the pros and cons of external ear lobes versus no ear lobes	2
make a chart	of different animals, their ear positions, and ear size	any number
measure	several different external auditory canals and compare sizes and shapes	any number
question	create a "know?-like to know?-learned?" about ears	3
research	problems and solutions for hearing needs of animals with poor eyesight	2
show cause and effect	of size of ear lobe for retaining and losing heat, possibly looking at elephants, polar bears, fennec fox, or jackrabbit	any number

Touch: Skin

Skill	Activity Suggestion	Foldable Parts
compare and contrast	eccrine and apocrine sweat glands	2
describe	the purposes of skin, including preventing fluid loss, defense against disease, protection from the Sun, protection from harmful substances, and regulation of body temperature	any number
determine	the purpose of sweat glands and sweat	1
diagram	the layers of human skin, including epidermis, dermis, and subcutaneous tissue	3
	epidermis layers of skin, including horny, granular, spinous, and basal	4
explain	the cause and effect of melanin in skin	2
	dandruff as the scalp shedding skin	1
graph	an estimation of world population by skin color	any number
observe	how nerve endings in the dermis respond to heat, cold, and touch	3
prove	the statement "Skin is the largest body organ."	1
question	create a "know?-like to know?-learned?" about skin	3
research	tactile nerves as they relate to whiskers on cats or rats, tails of moles, and fingers of humans	3
	how blood vessels in the dermis help regulate temperature	1
	the glands in the skin, including sebaceous oil and sweat	2
	the purpose of subcutaneous tissue, including fuel stored in fat cells, retention of heat, protection of internal tissues from external pressures, etc.	any number
	skin color	1
	melanocytes in the epidermis as they relate to skin color, freckles, and age spots	3
	different thicknesses of animal skin	any number
	keratin as it relates to animal skin	1
	how much and how frequently human skin is shed and replaced	1

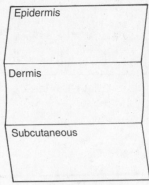

Trifold book

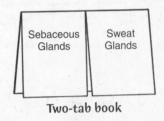

Two-tab book

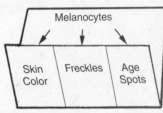

Concept-map book

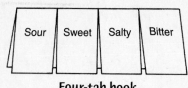

Four-tab book

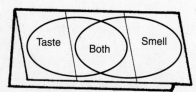

Three-tab Venn diagram

Bound-book journal

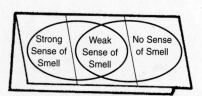

Three-tab Venn diagram

Person	Like	Dislike
D.Z.		
I.S.H.		
M.N.		

Folded table

Taste: Mouth and Tongue

Skill	Activity Suggestion	Foldable Parts
chart	taste likes and dislikes	2
compare and contrast	kinds of taste, possibly including sour, sweet, salty, and bitter	2 to 4
describe	form and function of the tongue, including taste, moving food, speech or calls, catching food, lapping, and cleaning fur	any number
design an experiment	to test the areas of taste on the tongue	any number
diagram	a taste bud	1
explain	how taste and smell are related	2
question	create a "know?-like to know?-learned?" about taste	3
research	the purpose of the papillae on the surface of the tongue	1
	saliva production, including parotid gland, sublingual, and submandibular	3
sequence	what happens internally when something is tasted	any number

Smell: Nose

Skill	Activity Suggestion	Foldable Parts
compare and contrast	animals with and without a nose	2
	animals with a strong sense of smell, animals with an underdeveloped sense of smell, and animals with no sense of smell	3
describe	nose purposes, including breathing, smelling, and moisturizing air moving into lungs	any number
diagram	the path of a breath of air, including nostrils, nasal passages, pharynx, trachea, and lungs	5
graph	sizes of different animal noses	any number
list	pros and cons of a strong sense of smell	2
make a chart	of different animals, their nose positions, nose size, dependence upon their sense of smell, and others	any number
question	create a "know?-like to know?-learned?" about noses	3
research	different-shaped noses and their purposes	any number
	animals with unusual noses, possibly including elephants or proboscis monkeys	any number
sequence	the internal and external events that are associated with the sense of smell, including olfactory nerve receptors, olfactory nerve fibers, and the olfactory bulb in the brain	any number
show cause and effect	of the sense of smell as it relates to taste	2

Systems

Circulatory System

Skill	Activity Suggestion	Foldable Parts
compare and contrast	arteries, veins, and capillaries	3
	superior vena cava and inferior vena cava	2
	systemic and pulmonary circulation	2
describe	blood as a liquid plasma and solid particles	2
diagram	the circulatory system, including heart, blood vessels, blood, and lymphatic system	4
examine	the purposes of the human circulatory system, including how it supplies body cells with food and oxygen and carries away carbon dioxide and waste, it regulates body temperature, it carries cells that help protect the body from disease, and it carries hormones	4
explain	why blood is circulated, including to transport food, carry oxygen, remove waste, carry disease-fighting organisms, and to carry hormones	any number
	the cause and effect of heart disease	2
identify	blood solids, including red blood cells, white blood cells, and platelets	3
illustrate	the form and function of the human heart	2
infer	why elephants have large ears and polar bears have small ears	1
question	create a "know?-like to know?-learned?" about circulatory system	3 3
research	animals with two-, three-, and four-chambered hearts	3
	the lymphatic system	1
	the purpose of valves in a heart	1
	the composition of blood, solids, and liquids	2
	the "who, what, when, where" of Christiaan Barnard	4

Excretory System

Skill	Activity Suggestion	Foldable Parts
describe	how urine is formed	1
diagram	the urinary system, including kidneys, ureter tubes, urinary bladder, and urethra	4
explain	the purpose of the excretory system	1
	the form and function of the kidneys	2
	cause and effect of urinating frequently	2
	the form and function of the bladder	2
question	create a "know?-like to know?-learned?" about the excretory system	3
research	nephrons, including Bowman's capsule, glomerulus, and tubule	3

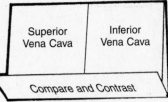

Two-tab matchbook

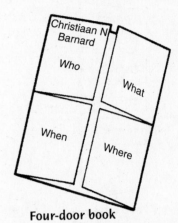

Four-door book

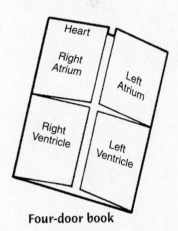

Four-door book

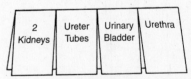

Four-tab book

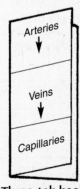

Three-tab book

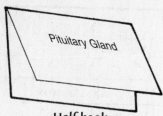

Half book

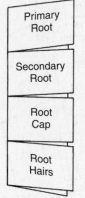

Four-tab book

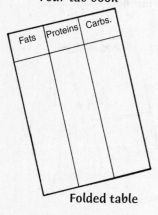

Folded table

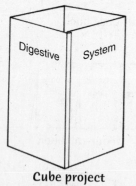

Cube project

Alimentary Canal
Mouth
Esophagus
Stomach
Small Intestine
Large Intestine
Rectum
Vocabulary

Layered book
(4 sheets of paper)

Endocrine System

Skill	Activity Suggestion	Foldable Parts
compare and contrast	endocrine glands and exocrine glands	2
describe	the function of the hypothalamus gland	1
	exocrine glands' function, including tears, sweat, mucus, and digestive juices	4
discuss	how animals that do not sweat deal with heat, such as panting	1
explain	how hormones are distributed	1
predict	what would happen if a human could not sweat	1
question	create a "know?-like to know?-learned?" about the endocrine system	3
research	the glands that regulate body functions, including growth, reproduction, food use, and stress and crisis	4
	three hormones, possibly including insulin, epinephrine, or oxytocin	3
	the main endocrine glands, including adrenal, pituitary, parathyroid, sex, and thyroid	5
	pituitary gland	1

Digestive System

Skill	Activity Suggestion	Foldable Parts
compare and contrast	small intestine and large intestine	2
define	chyme	1
describe	why chewing is important to good digestion	1
	the digestion of fats, proteins, and carbohydrates	3
diagram	the digestive system, including alimentary canal, gall bladder, liver, pancreas, salivary glands, and teeth	6
discuss	the statement "Water does not need to be digested."	1
explain	the importance of pancreatic juice, intestinal juice, and bile to digestion in the small intestine	3
list	the purposes of the digestive system, including breaking down food, absorption, and eliminating waste	3
make	a working model of a stomach, possibly using a plastic bag to show churning motion	any number
outline	how completely digested food is absorbed and used	any number
question	create a "know?-like to know?-learned?" about the digestive system	3
research	saliva	1
	the digestive juices, including enzymes, pH, and point of origin	3
	gastric juices	1
	how the gallbladder and pancreas aid digestion	2
	the importance of roughage in a diet	1
	coprolites	1

Integumentary System

Skill	Activity Suggestion	Foldable Parts
compare and contrast	eccrine and apocrine sweat glands	2
describe	the purposes of skin, including prevention of fluid loss, defense against disease, protection from the Sun, protection from harmful substances, and regulation of body temperature	any number
determine	the purpose of sweat glands and sweat	1
diagram	the layers of human skin, including epidermis, dermis, and subcutaneous tissue	3
	epidermis layers of skin, including horny, granular, spinous, and basal	4
explain	the cause and effect of melanin in skin	2
	dandruff as the scalp shedding skin	1
graph	an estimation of world population by skin color	any number
observe	how nerve endings in the dermis respond to heat, cold, and touch	3
prove	the statement "Skin is the largest body organ."	1
question	create a "know?-like to know?-learned?" about skin	3
research	tactile nerves as they relate to whiskers on cats or rats, tails of moles and fingers of humans	3
	how blood vessels in the dermis help regulate temperature	1
	the glands in the skin, including sebaceous oil and sweat	2
	the purpose of subcutaneous tissue, including fuel stored in fat cells, helps retain heat, protects internal tissues from external pressures	any number
	skin color	1
	melanocytes in the epidermis as they relate to skin color, freckles, and age spots	3
	different thicknesses of animal skin	any number
	keratin as it relates to animal skin	1
	how much and how frequently human skin is shed and replaced	1

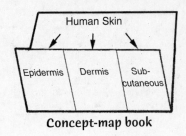

Concept-map book

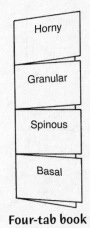

Four-tab book

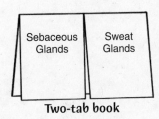

Two-tab book

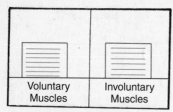

Voluntary Muscles | Involuntary Muscles

Pocket book

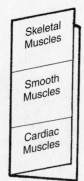

Skeletal Muscles

Smooth Muscles

Cardiac Muscles

Three-tab book

Muscular System

Skill	Activity Suggestion	Foldable Parts
compare and contrast	animals with and without a muscular system	2
	skeletal, smooth, and cardiac muscles	3
	voluntary and involuntary muscles	2
describe	how muscle strength can be increased	1
diagram	the form and function of muscle tissue	2
explain	how muscles help animals deal with the force of gravity	1
graph	how much muscle makes up an adult's body weight	2
hypothesize	how muscle systems of extinct animals can be reconstructed	1
identify	the muscle of red meat, chicken, and fish	3
make a Venn diagram	labeled *smooth muscle, skeletal muscle,* and *cardiac muscle*	3
observe	the movement of muscles in an animal	any number
question	create a "know?-like to know?-learned?" about the muscular system	3
research	the two largest groups of muscles (skeletal and smooth)	2
	the cardiac muscle	1
	a weight-training program	1
	the causes and effects of musculatory diseases	2
	the cause and effect of muscle atrophy	2
summarize	what happens when muscles get tired	any number

Nervous System

Skill	Activity Suggestion	Foldable Parts
compare and contrast	organisms with and without nervous systems	2
	the nervous systems in vertebrates and invertebrates	2
describe	the central nervous system, including the brain and spinal cord	2
determine	how nervous systems act as regulators, including digestion and breathing	any number
diagram	the human nervous system, including brain, spinal cord, and nerves	3
	the human brain, including cerebrum, cerebellum, and brain stem	3
explain	the purpose of a nervous system	1
	how humans react to stimuli, possibly including heat, cold, or fear	any number
graph	the percentage of the cerebrum to the rest of the brain (85%)	2
make a timeline	outlining our understanding of the nervous system	any number
outline	the main divisions of the nervous system, including central, peripheral, and autonomic nervous system	3
question	create a "know?-like to know?-learned?" about the nervous system	3
relate	a nervous system to a highway system	2
research	neurons, nerves, and nerve network	3
	form and function of a neuron, including axon, cell body, and dendrites	3
	the peripheral nervous system, including sensory neurons, association neurons, and motor neurons	3
	the autonomic nervous system and what it regulates, possibly including heart beat or food movement	any number
	autonomic nervous system, including sympathetic and parasympathetic systems	2
	how the human brain differs from the brains of other animals	2

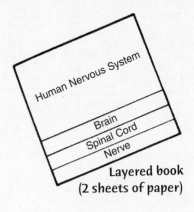

Layered book
(2 sheets of paper)

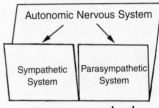

Concept-map book

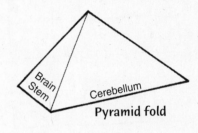

Pyramid fold

Lymphatic System

Skill	Activity Suggestion	Foldable Parts
compare and contrast	lymph to blood	2
describe	the form and function of the lymphatic system	2
	five organs that have lymphatic vessels, including skin, liver, heart, lungs, and intestines	5
explain	how and why the lymphatic system returns interstitial fluids to the bloodstream	2
question	create a "know?-like to know?-learned?" about the lymphatic system	3
research	lymphatic vessels, lymph, lymph nodes, lymphocytes, and lymphoid tissue	5
	how lymphocytes and macrophages help fight infection	1
	Hodgkin's disease	1

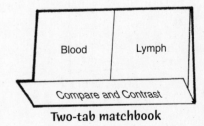

Two-tab matchbook

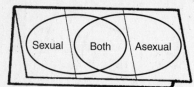

Three-tab Venn diagram

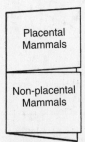

Two-tab book

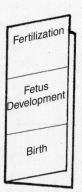

Folded table

Reproductive System

Skill	Activity Suggestion	Foldable Parts
compare and contrast	sexual and asexual reproduction	2
	placentals and nonplacentals	2
define	fertilization	1
describe	mammal reproduction, including placentals, marsupials, and monotremes	3
	the female reproductive system, including ovaries, Fallopian tubes, uterus, vagina, and vulva	5
explain	the male reproductive system, including testicles, duct system, glands, and penis	4
	the form and function of ovaries	2
make a Venn diagram	labeled *sexual reproduction, asexual reproduction,* and *both*	3
outline	fertilization, fetus development, and birth of human baby	3
question	create a "know?-like to know?-learned?" about the reproductive system	3
research	reproduction in placental mammals, including fertilization, development in uterus, attachment to placenta, and nourishment through placenta	any number
	sperm and egg reproduction	2
	sperm production	1
	menstrual cycle and menstruation	2
	different gestation periods, possibly including humans, cattle, hamsters, and elephants	any number

Three-tab book

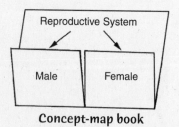

Concept-map book

Respiratory System

Skill	Activity Suggestion	Foldable Parts
compare and contrast	right lung with three lobes and left lung with two lobes	2
	respiratory systems in land and water animals	2
describe	the function of the respiratory system, including providing oxygen and ridding body of carbon dioxide	1
	the purpose of the nasal passages, including filtering dust, warming air, and moistening air	any number
determine	the cause and effect of bronchitis	2
diagram	the human respiratory organs, including nose, trachea, and lungs	3
	the path of air movement through the body, including nose, nasal passages, pharynx, larynx, trachea, and lungs	6
explain	the process of inhaling and exhaling	2
	purposes of the pulmonary artery and veins	2
illustrate	the respiratory cycle	2
	the function of primary bronchi, bronchioles, terminal bronchioles, and alveoli	4
question	create a "know?-like to know?-learned?" about the respiratory system	3

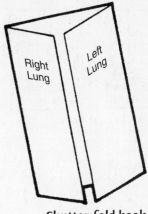

Shutter-fold book

Three-tab book

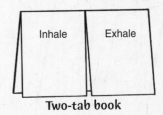

Two-tab book

Skeletal System

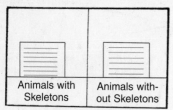

Pocket book

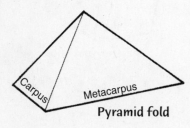

Pyramid fold

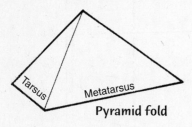

Pyramid fold

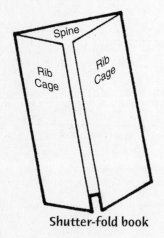

Shutter-fold book

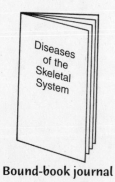

Bound-book journal

Skill	Activity Suggestion	Foldable Parts
compare and contrast	animals with and without a skeletal system	2
	the bones of a human baby and an adult	2
	the bones of the shoulder and arm to levers	2
	movable joints and fixed joints	2
	the human skeleton and that of another vertebrate	2
define	a joint	1
determine	what percentage the skull is to the height of an average adult	1
diagram	arm bones, including scapula, clavicle, humerus, radius, and ulna	5
	leg bones, including pelvic girdle, femur, tibia, and fibula	4
	the spinal column, including 7 cervical vertebrae, 12 thoracic vertebrae, and 5 lumbar vertebrae	3
examine	two types of body movement (skeletal and musculatory)	2
graph	the number of vertebrae, cervical, thoracic, and lumbar	3
list	the hand bones, including carpus, metacarpus, and phalanges	3
	the foot bones, including tarsus, metatarsus, and phalanges	3
observe	skeletons as a supportive framework and protection for organs	2
	the importance of the 12 ribs on each side of the body	2
question	create a "know?-like to know?-learned?" about the skeletal system	3
research	the human skeleton, including axial and appendicular	2
	adult pelvic girdle or hip bones	1
	the bones in the hands and feet	1
	how long it takes bone to become petrified	1
	cause and effect of diseases of the skeletal system	2
sequence	the events of bone fossilization	any number
summarize	the importance of bone cells, including how they produce new blood cells and regulate mineral content of blood	2

Index